BRAND IDENTITY

BUILDING YOUR BREAKTHROUGH BUSINESS WITH BRANDING PAYS

SHELDON LEONARD

Copyright © 2019 by Sheldon Leonard

All rights reserved.

No part of this book may be reproduced in any form or by any electronic or mechanical means, including information storage and retrieval systems, without written permission from the author, except for the use of brief quotations in a book review.

Some people dream of success, while other people get up every morning and make it happen.

— *Wayne Huizenga, owner of Blockbuster Video and the Miami Dolphins*

BRAND IDENTITY

CONTENTS

Introduction ix

1. Developing Your Brand's Purpose 1
2. A Guide to Getting People to Turn Their Heads 19
3. How to Begin to Build Your Brand Among Your Customers 40
4. Keeping the Customer on the Hook 56
5. Sealing the Deal 71
6. The Secret Way to Make Sure Your Brand is Never Sitting Still or Falling Behind 86

Conclusion 101

INTRODUCTION

I want to thank you and congratulate you for downloading *Brand Identity: Building Your Breakthrough Business with Branding Pays!*

How do you want your customers to see you? What do you want them to think about as a first impression? And how can you create this impression or perception? The answer is through your brand identity. And a few of the components that make up your identity include the "tone" of voice you use, the name of your business, graphics, colors, and shapes, including your logo. This may sound a lot like your image, but it is different. An image is the result of your identity efforts. This means that if you succeed in developing a brand identity, you will able to generate a positive image.

Think about brands that are universally recognizable. These are the brands with a strong brand identity. Large companies spend millions and even billions on developing this identity because they understand how there is a strong connection to the market share they own and their sales flow. To help you further, consider the Nike swoosh symbol and how even children recognize the brand and can recall their main messages. Or consider the apple with a bite out of it for Apple. When someone sees this logo, they begin to connect the brand to a personality and identity. But it's not all about the logo. Coca-Cola is another strong brand identity, and while they do have a logo, it is the image of red and white with bubbles that can say, "Coca-Cola" before anything else.

You may not have millions of dollars to invest in developing your brand or want to corner a big piece of your market, but building a strong brand identity is important. Some of the benefits any business, any size can capitalize on include:

1. You can develop a price premium. This is a way to get customers to spend more for something just because of the brand. People are willing to pay more for a brand all on its own, and you can be one of those brands if you put in the work. Even a small business shows your customers that you offer quality that is worth the higher price.
2. Quality is in the perception you create. If a customer pays more for something, they perceive that your brand is giving them the quality that is worth the extra cost. It is not always true, but it is the perception. To do this, you can simply make your brand look like a higher quality than your competition, even if your products are similar.
3. You raise awareness and loyalty. If a person can remember your brand, they are more likely to come back to do business with you again. A good way to help them remember you is to develop a strong identity. In

addition, it is important for your customers to be associated with a "good" brand, and are more likely to recommend you to their friends and family, if they have a good impression about your brand.
4. Customers see you are reliable and experienced. Investing in your identity helps customers see you as a business worth paying attention to. A strong identity helps create the appearance of a well-established brand that has been around for a long time. In addition, a strong identity helps customers see you as trustworthy and reliable, especially compared to brands in your market that do not have a brand. Also, an identity opens the door to collaborations with larger companies, if you are a business-to-business brand. It is one of the best ways to get noticed by the big players in your market or your target audience.
5. One effective way to set yourself apart is differentiating your brand from the other players in the market, and it is a continuous struggle. One of the best places to start to make your brand stand out is through a strong identity. Part of this differentiation is achieved through your perceived quality, which in turn leads to higher prices and so on. If you are a small brand, you can use a strong identity to rise above the other competition, even larger businesses, meaning you get more business and profits in the long run.

It is clear that a place to build and grow your brand is through your brand's identity. You can bring in more and bigger business, can bring in the business that you really want for your brand, and you can shape your success from the center rather than superficial. The chapters in this book are your guide to developing your identity through various places, and also offer suggestions on how to develop and re-develop your brand from infancy through success. The tips in this book will be there for you from the start and grow with your brand as you navigate the ever-changing landscape of brand identity.

The purpose of this book is to provide you a guide for creating a brand identity that will succeed over time and provide actionable tips you can apply today to enhance your identity, even if it has been around for years. This is not just a book about theory and concept, but rather a tool to teach you how to boost your brand and truly benefit from branding. The chapters also address different stages of business and brand development so you can apply concepts according to your own lifecycle as appropriate. Consider this the branding tool that you can go back to, time and time again, to improve your presence in your market.

As you begin this journey, I want to thank you again for downloading this book. I hope you find it informative and enjoy it!

1

DEVELOPING YOUR BRAND'S PURPOSE

Before you put your brand out to the world, it is important to define how you will bring life to your brand in a compelling and clear manner. This helps you grow with relevance while still being different from your competition. An approach like this is what can make the difference between "making it" and failing. But before you can begin making your brand stand out, you need to know exactly what a brand's purpose is.

A simple way to think of your brand's purpose is that it is the "why" your brand exists, beyond just making a profit. A brand must be able to explain what it offers and how it will be delivered, but the way to make it stand out is why it is offering it to the market. This is the reason you are operating this business and essential to establishing a strong brand. Making money is the result of your brand, not the purpose of it. This means you need to know the true reason your brand exists, and all your employees should know this purpose, too.

To illustrate the difference between the "What," "How," and

"Why," is Tesla. The car company designs a line of vehicles that are powered by electricity rather than fuel. They accomplish this task by fostering an innovative and progressive culture in design and technology. Why they do it is to move the world forward towards a more sustainable transportation method. For the CEO, Elon Musk, it is not about working hard to make money, but rather working hard for a cause. He explains that working towards the mission of Tesla is easy. And he easily shares this purpose with the employees of Tesla, who all understand the value of the work they are doing for the betterment of the global climate, as well as the customers who purchase a Tesla vehicle. This is a great example of a clear and defined brand and the brand's purpose.

There is a large difference between the mission and vision of a brand and its purpose. Sadly, in the world of business, there is no clear definition of "brand purpose." In addition, there is no clear path for turning that purpose into actionable steps. This leads many people to confuse the vision and the mission with the purpose of the brand. However, there are important differences between the three of them. Because there is no accepted distinction between the three currently, the following is a combination of various concepts and parameters to offer an explanation for your developmental purposes:

- Purpose: Again, this is the deeper "why" for your business to exist. It goes beyond making money or your shareholders happy. It is what drives you to bring this brand to the world.
- Mission: This statement describes "what" you are going to do to get to your goals or vision. This should

be clear steps or initiatives you plan to take to achieve your plans.
- Vision: Your vision statement is "where" you see your brand going in the next few years. It is your goal for the company.

An additional term you must understand in relation to "purpose," "mission," and "vision," is "values." Values describe "how" you want your employees, shareholders, board members, and even customers to act so you can fulfill your mission, vision, and purpose. This term guides your people in how they should behave as they take steps to reach for the future and stay aligned with the purpose of the brand. You can think of these four terms like a bullseye. The center of it all is the purpose of your brand. It is the soul of why you exist in the first place. From there, the next ring consists of where you want to go in the future or your vision. The third ring in the bullseye is how you plan to reach those future goals and stay focused on your purpose; meaning the third ring is your mission. Finally, your values surround the bullseye, offering the behaviors and qualities you want everyone to embrace to be able to pull off everything inside of the target.

In the marketing world, there are four "P's." These pillars make up a brand and must clearly be defined before anything can be delivered to the public. These four "P's" include "product," "price," "placement," and "promotion."

1. Product - This defines what you are making or offering.
2. Price - The cost of the product must be set based on profit goals, etc.

3. Placement - Your customers interact and purchase things through different channels, depending on what product they are buying and the price they are willing to spend. You need to know how you are going to get your products to them so they can purchase it in a place that makes sense.
4. Promotion - Marketing the item is the fourth pillar that is critical to making sure your customers understands the brand and products.

But are these four pillars really enough for a business to succeed in today's market? The answer is no. It is increasingly important for a business to stand out from one another and to have a reason for existing in the first place. This is why marketing education and application must include a fifth pillar, the pillar of purpose. The purpose is a foundational requirement for a brand, and without a clearly defined purpose, you cannot really make a decision about the primary four pillars without it.

Examples of Clear Brand Purpose

It is important your brand's purpose extends to every person in your company and to your customers. It does not matter if the person is unclogging a toilet, scanning ID badges, or sitting in the corner office. The purpose of the company should be known and embraced by all. A few brands that set forth clear distinctions about their purpose include:

- Zappos – "Delivering Happiness."
- Walmart – "Saving people money so they can live better."

- Coca-cola – "To refresh the world ... To inspire moments of optimism and happiness."
- Google – "Make [the world's] information universally accessible and useful."
- Starbucks – "To inspire and nurture the human spirit…"
- Nike – "To bring inspiration and innovation to every athlete. If you have a body, you are an athlete."

Notice how these statements from these brands do not discuss the products they offer or the ways they are going to deliver these things. It does not talk about how they will do this in the future, but rather offers the deeper meaning for their brand. It is the foundation that all the other pillars stand upon.

The Importance of Purpose

This is not merely conjecture. It is backed up by fact and reality. In the book "Grow" by Proctor and Gamble's previous CMO, Jim Stengel, he reveals how that out of more than 50,000 brands studied, the top 50 of the highest-performing brands were driven by purpose, or as Stengel called it, "ideals." And over the ten-year study, Stengel observed that these 50 businesses also experienced faster growth than their competition to the tune of three times faster. In addition, Keith Weed, the CMO of Unilever, proclaimed that the brands that perform the highest in their portfolio are those that are founded on a purpose. The CEO of Unilever, Paul Polman, agrees with the importance of having a solid purpose, explaining that brands with a clear purpose have "values that drive their value."

And beyond the bottom line, purpose also plays a role in

recruiting talent for your business. Today, people no longer just want to clock in and clock out, not having valued contributions or belief in the company they work for. Employees want to know that what they provide supports something larger and that they believe deeper meaning to their workplace. They want to be a "part of something larger." This means more than just making a profit for the company. This opinion is strong within the "Millennial" generation, but before you discount it for more experienced workers, other generational groups identify with this mindset as well, including Generation Z. This alone should illustrate the importance of having a clear purpose. But if you do not want to believe the surveys conducted on thousands of people around the United States, think about it from a personal level. Would you rather work for a business that impacts society in a meaningful way or one solely focused on making money? Chances are, you are not the only one with your opinion on the matter.

Types of Brand Purpose

Not all purposes are "created equal." There are some primary classifications for a brand's purpose, which can aid you in determining your own brand's deep-set "why."

The five classifications are:

1. Societal impact: A "change" is needed in society, and you can offer one such solution. This can be through pushing back on the "norms" of society, reclassifying perspectives on hot-button topics, or broadly looking to better society. Think of brands like Dove or IBM.
2. Instill pride: A brand that makes their employees and customers proud to own it is doing something right on both ends. They make people feel vital and confident

when they work or use a certain brand. Think of brands like Mercedes-Benz.
3. Promote adventure and exploration: Venturing beyond the well-traveled path or finding your "legs" allows you to enjoy new experiences. It also opens up new perspectives on topics or locations. Think of brands like Pampers, Discovery, and Airbnb.
4. Fostering connection: Bringing people together in a variety of ways, including connecting them with each other and the world in general. Think of brands like Starbucks, Nike, and FedEx.
5. Bring joy to others: Sometimes, you just want to make people happy. You want them to feel joyful, childlike, and in wonder. Think of brands like Coca-cola and Zappos.

Your brand may fall under one category or a mix of one or more, but try to select your niche purpose so you can build a strong foundation for your brand. Be careful, however, of falling into the trap of thinking your purpose can only be cause-related or socially acceptable ideas. They can be, but do not have to be. What really matters is that your brand exudes itself in every action you take with your brand. All things, including the standard four "P's" outlined earlier, should reinforce the idea of your brand's purpose. Additionally, do not become too attached to your purpose. It can mold with the times and the changes. Sometimes the change exists in a single word, while other times it can be a complete alteration of the purpose of the brand. For example, Tesla changed from "sustainable transport," to "sustainable energy," in an effort to reflect the brand's movement from just vehicles to energy sources in general.

It is important that you take the time to define your brand's purpose. As you set out to develop a new brand, you have the best opportunity to determine the initial purpose. It is more challenging to define a purpose for an established brand, especially if it has been around for decades without a clear purpose to embrace, but it is important to discover the brand's purpose. There are a few ways to find this including:

- Dig into the heritage and history of the brand. If you have a brand that has been around for a long time, there is a wealth of information available about who and what the brand is. You can research the founder's, the reason they created the brand, and more. Using the research you uncover, you can distill a purpose from the past that still threads through to the present. For new brands, that heritage is not there. This means you need to find the reasons that you are developing this brand and use that to begin defining the purpose.
- The evolution of the idea and brand. Sometimes a new brand has gone through a variety of changes before landing where it is. Products and prices and target markets are all tossed around until something starts to settle. This is all relevant to defining the purpose. In addition, as a brand age, it begins to change. These changes should align with the brand's purpose and core meaning.
- Evaluate your passion and the strength of the brand. In other words, consider what you love doing and what you are good at and what you recognize as a need in your community. If all three of these things were to intersect, this is what you can bring to the world that

has meaning to others and to yourself. Essentially, this is your brand's purpose.
- For established companies and brands, talk to the people on the ground. Find out from employees and even customers what they think the purpose of the brand is. Ask for stories about how they engage with the brand. Find out why they are proud to work for that company or buy those products. If your brand is large and spans across the globe, you can still elicit feedback that can be crucial to uncovering the perceived value of the brand.

You should use a combination of these tips to create a strong purpose for your brand, and when you do, you need to bring it to life. But the process of bringing a purpose to life is not always easy. To begin, you need to establish this purpose in the culture of your company. Your employees must stand behind the definition of purpose because they are the ones breathing life into what you offer. There is nothing more powerful than a team of people supporting your purpose. If they believe in what you are founded upon, they will "live" that purpose and bring it to your customers.

Finding Your Niche

Being "generic" or "vague" is a death sentence to almost every brand out there, including yours. Your customers have a choice to go with you or choose someone who is bold and individual. If your purpose does not stand out to them, they will go with someone who does. This is a great way to establish your "competitive edge" in your field. A great way to do this is to find a niche that your competition has not already gobbled up. To do this, you need to be savvy and aware of the market. Below are tips on how to do this:

1. Research your market — a lot. When you start a business, you probably spent a good amount of time looking into your market and defining who they are. This means, if you are just starting out, you are in a good spot. But if you have been in business for a year or more, it is time to re-look at who your market is and what they are doing. Sometimes your market has changed since you started. For example, you may have gathered a core group of loyal customers, but now they are in a different phase of their life and no longer align with your brand's purpose and offerings. This means you need to shift your purpose to re-align with these changes or find a way to shift to a different customer base. You will only be able to decide this once you define and re-examine your market.
2. Practice introspection. This is more than just looking in at what you want, but additionally at who you want to work with and what you want to offer them. Maybe you want to reach a certain group of people in a specific spot or age range. Sometimes it is another demographic or socio-economic factor you want to target. Be honest and real about what you want.
3. Cut it down to size. Big companies have big markets. Small companies thrive in niches. This means you need to par down your reach and focus in on those that matter to your overall purpose and mission. Find out who these people are and cater to their needs and desires. Get really good at giving them what they want. Think about the following business niches that are

thriving today. A cleaning business that eliminates used gum from places it has been unwittingly stuck. Online stores that offer products that are wooden or non-electrical for those that want a more simple or "healthy" lifestyle. Salons that target working women who are busy that have just a few minutes to come in for a wash and style.

4. Shop, or just browse, your competition. This does not mean you should become one of the best customers for a competitor, but it does mean that you should be on their mailing list, follow their marketing strategies, and know their product offering. You should also have a good idea of who their target market is and their foundational purpose. When you have a good idea of what they are offering, you also identify what they are leaving on the table for you to pick up. But what if there are a lot of competitors? This means not only do you need to know all about all of them, but you also have to think long and hard if there is any room for you at the table in the first place.

5. Give your customer a name and personality. Make up the "ideal" customer or group of customers that will shop your brand. Give them a name, personality traits, hobbies, etc. You can even give them a face! Sometimes you have more than one "perfect" customer, in which case you should spend time clearly defining who these people are so you can start determining how you will message your brand to each one individually. A few examples of brand personas include Jim, a retired city worker, likes trying out different cuisines but has trouble or does not like to leave his home to go to a restaurant. Jen is a hip, youthful professional woman

putting in long hours at her job so when she makes it home, she does not want to go out to eat or even cook at home. Sam is a single, working father who wants to feed his kids a healthy meal but does not have a lot of time to spend on prepping for it.

6. Make adjustments as needed. It is important that once you do all your research that you choose a single niche market. Make sure that however you decide to "fine-tune" your niche that you have good reasons for doing so. And as the market changes, you adjust to those changes for good reasons, as well.

7. Adjust your branding as well. The messages you are putting out needs to reflect your current niche market. This means that if you adjust your market in any way, your messaging needs to adjust, too. The same goes for changes to your purpose. If you tweak your purpose, you need to tweak your messaging. A good message should speak to your customer and accurately share information about your brand. If you are not sure about how effective your message is, gather a focus group, send out surveys, or poll people on social media. You can also pilot variations of messaging on different platforms and see which ones are responded to the best.

The reason for defining and developing around your purpose and niche is to make your brand stand out. Your accuracy and a narrowed definition will make you memorable and successful.

Striking the Fine-line Balance

You have two goals in business when it comes to your brand. You want to be a pillar in your market but also distinctive.

Pillars, or central brands, such as McDonald's or Coca-Cola, are the brands that others compare themselves to. They are some of the "first" mentioned when talking about their market. Their presence sets the dynamics of a category. All of these dynamics include innovation, pace, prices, and even the preferences of customers. On the other hand, brands that are distinct do not directly compete with another because they are so different. They are the ones that "stand out" from all the others in their market. Think of brands like Dos Equis and Tesla. But balancing between the two is vital.

What you choose to do and portray infiltrates how you are perceived, how much will be sold, and the price you can charge. In addition, this directly determines your bottom line. Before, brands struggled to gather the information necessary to do this. It was a challenge to analyze the performance of the brand in relation to the position of the brand. Historically, the brand position was placed on a map, highlighting how a consumer felt on either side of a concept. On the other hand, performance was historically assessed by a linear measurement of profitability, a rate of growth, and share of the market.

But now there is a new map that shows the distinction of a brand as well as its proximity to pillar status. With a map like this, you can now compare a position with price and sales. Using this tool lets you decide where to place resources, make strategic decisions, watch the performance in regard to competition over time, and determine the performance of the strategy in relation to the results plotted. A process like this aligns pillar and distinction like never before. This way, you can decide how close or far you want to be from one or the other.

Like any analysis, it is important to recognize that it is easy to create; however, it does take time. To begin, you must recognize the geographic area of interest and the targeted group of customers in that area. These two points of interest determine the brand's map position. Once these primary points are defined, surveys related to the brand's pillar status or distinctions are delivered. These surveys score the brand from zero to ten on both topics and are given to consumers to respond to. Using a matrix of two by two, the information from the surveys will plot the position of the brand. When you place the dot on the matrix, adjust the size according to a metric like a price or sales volume.

Doing mapping this way also allows you to determine how the brand looks across geographical locations and even categories. It allows you the opportunity to determine if the market has too many of one type of brand versus another. This is a good way to determine the profitability, risk, pricing, and sales for a particular brand.

- Like similar maps, when a brand falls into a specific quadrant, it is designated as a certain "kind" of the brand. For example, in this potential map, those placed into the quadrant on the right top, can be considered "aspirational." This means that they are a "powerhouse" for the market. They are very distinct and can charge a higher price than their competition. If your brand is appealing but not distinct, it will be on the right but the lower quadrant. These can be considered "mainstream." When your customers think of the market, these are the brands they think of. The lower prices help drive sales, but customers will continue to buy them because of their reputation and lower costs, maintaining a steady revenue stream.

On the other hand, if a brand is not distinguishable, they struggle with not being the first "choice" or "consideration" for a customer. These "peripheral" brands fall into the lower quadrant on the left side of the map. It may sound strange, but having low prices and a low level of distinction can still result in a successful brand. It just may be harder than other combinations. The final quadrant located on the top to the left are brands that are "unconventional." These brands offer something unique to the market that sets them apart from the "normal" options. This is a good place to be if you have the "right" uniqueness, but it is a very niche group you will be marketing to, meaning sales will be lower, so prices need to be higher.

This is all well and good to look at on a map, but how does this translate to the dollars and cents of the business? Well, when something is more "central," it tends to have the best sales. The more you can nudge your brand to the center of the map, the more sales you can expect. Even moving it one point on the surveys can create a dramatic peak in your volume. On paper, this sounds simple, but you know this is not always easy or cost-effective. However, it is something to keep in the back of your mind as you work on determining how and where your brand sits.

As could be deduced from the information in the previous paragraph, the further you move away from the center of the map and become more "distinct," the lower your sales volume becomes. Moving out is not as dramatic as moving in terms of impact on your sales volume. However, it is valuable to recognize that this will most likely occur if you want a "distinct" brand instead of something more of a "pillar."

The impact of "centrality" on price does not necessarily directly correlate with the impact on volume. After all, why would any brand want to sacrifice sales volume just to be unique? It is because they can raise their prices, generate good revenue, and walk away with a profit with fewer products sold. The success of distinct brands lies in their pricing model. As you move your brand out from the center of your map, further into the "distinction" zone, you can correspond your movement with a price increase. Each point distance you move, determine how it will impact your pricing.

But what if you are moving inwards to become a "pillar?" The reduction in the price of your products is not as significant. It may be about 50% of the price increase going in the opposite direction. For example, if you were to move out one point and be more distinct, you would increase the price by $3, but if you were to move one point in towards the center, you would lower your price by $1.50.

Implications of Using This Mapping System

It is important to remember, that while choosing to map your brand this way can be a tremendous help and tool, it is also subject to change. If you alter your target market, geographical location, etc., the location of your brand on the map will change. In addition, if a new competitor enters your market, it will affect your location. What is important to recognize is if your brand falls into or close to the quadrant that reflects your purpose and goals. Your business model, mission, and vision should all align with how customers perceive you. If you are in a completely alternate quadrant than what you want, you need to take a long and hard look at how you are presenting your brand to the market.

Notes on each brand "type" include:

- Aspirational - These are brands that are considered both distinct and central. This is why they can charge a high price and also enjoy a high level of sales. These are brands customers "trust." They are also in the best position to introduce "new" concepts to the market that will be accepted by the general public. These brands "pave the way" for other brands in the same category and market. What brands in this grouping need to focus on is being distinct in a way that appeals to the masses but is not considered "run of the mill." These brands also have to defend themselves from encroaching unconventional and mainstream players constantly.
- Mainstream - Brands in this group are mostly centrally located. They are the brand's people think about when they think about a certain market, and it is mainly thanks to the heavy amount of advertising done by these brands. These brands typically avoid risks. They are big players, though, and are often credited with stamping out what customers want and buy. Unconventional and peripheral brands are the ones that challenge this group the most. The brands in these other quadrants can shift to become more "mainstream" if consumer preference shifts, making it important for mainstream brands always to be aligning with customer's "taste" early.
- Peripheral - Customers flock to this category because

the brand's products are similar to the central or aspirational products, but at a lower cost. These brands are the "substitutes" or "kind of like" options. The low level of engagement in the market and the low prices are what interest customers at this level. Keep in mind that this group does not have high levels of sales nor high prices. To make a successful business here, you must choose a market that requires little marketing or cost for innovation. These include industries like grocery and pharmaceuticals. If you settle into this sector, it is hard and expensive to get out. Most of the time, brands will simply exit the market if they get "stuck" here. On the other hand, keeping the business costs low can keep it successful. Just think of how RC Cola has been able to live on for almost 100 years.

- Unconventional - The niche brands settle into this quadrant. You must be able to offer a product that has a price point reflecting the expectation of lower sales volume. This is the only way to succeed in the niche, unconventional group. On the other hand, if your plan is to nudge closer to the center, you can use this as a place to start as you then offer something more central to the masses. One of the ways to become more central from here is to find ways to make the unique offerings more "mainstream" or bring in more "mainstream" ideas into the innovation. While centrality is attractive, movement from "unconventional" to "aspirational" is also an option and can maintain distinction and higher prices while increasing sales volume. Moving towards centrality will result in lower prices.

2

A GUIDE TO GETTING PEOPLE TO TURN THEIR HEADS

When you are coming up with an idea and brand, you can realize that it is not always that easy to figure out how to turn heads - in a good way. Everything matters when you think about your brand; the colors, the font, the imagery, and more. But before you start hyperventilating about the message all caps, all lower case or a combination sends, remember it is all about the broader perspective. This is not a time to panic, but rather some time to have conscious fun. Note the word, "conscious." As you read on, you will encounter some fun marketing had that was not very conscious of their messaging and it failed in a big way. The tips in this chapter are designed to help you avoid that! But to begin, take a look at what exactly a brand strategy is.

A quick definition of brand strategy is, "A plan that includes specific goals set for the long-term, which is achievable as the brand successfully evolves."

A brand that has a successful strategy finds a way to mix together the character of the company with its messages so customers can easily identify it. When it can do this, all parts of the business are impacted. And this strategy is closely tied to the competition as well as the emotions and needs of the customer. But remember, this is the "big picture" view. Your brand is so much more than just a product you are selling or the name of your business. Most of your brand is something you cannot touch or see; it is a feeling that you project through all sorts of things. To be able to define your brand in a single image or word is nearly impossible for most successful brands. This intangible messaging, the feeling that underlies all that you do, is what sets you apart as either a success and long-term player, or just another dot in the long line of mediocrity in the market.

To help you settle-in for the long term, the following suggestions below are designed to assist you in learning the "science" and the "art" of building a brand that can turn heads.

Suggestion 1: Everything starts with your purpose

Remember chapter 1? It is coming back here to remind you just how important it is. Your promise that you are making to the market originates from your purpose or the deeper reason for developing this brand in the first place. This purpose is what makes you different from the competition and valuable to your customers. It is why you get up in the morning, why your employees keep coming back to work, and why your customers want to buy from you. A generic promise is not enough; it needs to come from this deep-seated place.

Maybe your purpose is more functional in that it pinpoints a successful evaluation or more intentional in that it relates to the good that it provides to the market or community. While there is no right or wrong purpose in business, the brands with a more "intentional" purpose tend to have a stronger work environment and more loyal customers.

Think of IKEA and their vision, "... to create a better everyday life for the many people." Selling furniture is how they plan to provide this betterment, but the appeal of value beyond just a sofa or new chair is attractive to many people. IKEA is committing to its customers to help them better their lives, which really has nothing to do with their inexpensive table linens or Swedish meatballs. So as you come up with your purpose, remember to dig beyond the surface of what you are offering and go into the "why" you are doing it at all. This is a great place to start to make sure people are looking with admiration at your brand.

Suggestion 2: Stick to the Script

If a topic does not enhance your brand or relate to it in a clear way, stay away from it. You need to be consistent and somewhat predictable. Each time you put something out there, ask yourself if it aligns with your purpose and message. Cohesive, consistent, clear, concise are all great words to think about here. You do not want to confuse your stakeholders by throwing up a funny meme that does not fall in line with your brand. The great thing about consistency is that the longer you "stick to the script" and deliver a reliable message over and over, the more loyal customers you develop.

Think of Coca-cola and their commitment to their brand messaging. All their messages, images, etc., are in harmony. This harmony has to lead to its brand recognition worldwide. It is all about being consistent. To help your employees and others keep consistent, put together a "style guide." This helps people know the tone of voice to use in spoken our written communication in relation to the brand, to the exact colors that should be used in images. It can even delve into the positioning strategy for specific goods. This takes time to develop in the beginning, but the benefits, in the long run, are often worth it.

Suggestion 3: Bring Emotion Into It

Purchasing is not always a rational decision, even when purchasing necessities. People are emotional creatures, fueled by their collective experiences. This is why people will purchase something that is more expensive, even when there is a cheaper alternative with similar quality. Somewhere in the mental buying process and the emotional trigger was set off telling that person it was a better choice for them to spend more for whatever reason. And often that reason is a sense of community or belonging. A brand can bring people together in unique ways, such as wearing the same shoes as another person or driving the same make of a car as another person. There is pride in being a part of this brand's "tribe," if you take time to make it emotional.

Take Harley as an example. This brand has done a great job of linking their sense of community tightly to their brand. The Harley Owner's Group, or HOG, is an online social site for owners of their motorcycles to connect with one another as well as more "personally" with the brand. This simple feature on a website is a powerful way to make people decide to buy from you instead of a competitor. Even if it does not make sense for your brand to create a special social media site for your customers, you can still think of creative ways to connect with your customers on a more personal level. You can engage them more emotionally in some way. Offer a "peace of mind," welcome them to your "family," offer tools to help them live life a little easier.

Suggestion 4: Always Stretch Before a Workout

Before you make a move, you need to be flexible. The world is always changing, including your customers. This means you need to as well. Of course, this opens up a world of creativity for your business, but it also means you cannot just jump into a brand strategy with research and information you prepared months before or for something else. You need to "stretch" or research and prepare before moving or messaging. But now you may wonder, how can you be flexible but also consistent? I hope you are asking yourself this question because it is an important one! The balance you are looking to strike is familiarity and identification while also being relatable and fresh. This means that you may keep elements of your "old" brand but alter it in ways to reflect the changes of the "tide."

Think of the transition Old Spice has gone through. Before a few years ago, Old Spice was the deodorant of dad's and grandfather's, but no hip kid reached for a tube of it in public! But teaming up with a new creative marketing team, they came up with a new brand strategy that widened their customer base in a human and fresh way. Now almost any man of any age is not embarrassed to sport Old Spice, and many are proud users of the renovated brand. They did not throw all their history out though; you can still see the foundation of their logo, typography, and color scheme in there. It is not so wildly different that people do not associate the new with the old, but it is just an update that was needed for the strong brand.

Think about your brand and how you can "think outside the box." What ways can you engage your customers that you have not tried before? Is there something amazing about your brand or products that you can highlight that you have not showcased before? Changing your strategy when it stops working or does not work is ok. Just remember, you want to keep your loyal customers as well as attract new ones, so stay focused on balancing the flexibility with consistency every time.

Suggestion 5: Use Your Tools – Your Employees

One of your greatest assets, tools, and markers of success in branding is your employees. You can have the best style guide, strategy, and purpose, but if you forget about the importance of your employees in the mix, you are going to struggle. Your employees are often the ones facing your customers on a consistent basis or are engaging in your brand all the time. That means they need to really understand what your brand is all about and how you want to message it. Think about just a personality type. If your brand is stoic, conservative, serious, or classic, a customer would be confused if they went into a store where the employee they interacted with was aloof, goofy, or very contemporary. You do not want your customer to feel disconnected between your brand and your employees.

A great example of strong employee engagement is Zappos. No matter how a customer interacts with Zappos, their experience is human, helpful, and solid. In fact, Zappos has a department in their company dedicated to making sure the customer-employee interaction is aligned with the brand strategy. The department, titled "Zappos Insights," makes sure that all employees are aware of the company's core values and is committed to the brand.

· · ·

SUGGESTION 6: Show Your Loyalty

If they love you, show them love in return! If a customer keeps coming back to you, show them that you appreciate them. It may sound simple or obvious, but you would be surprised how many companies forget to do this. But these loyal customers are your community ambassadors. When you foster this commitment, you are actually developing a grassroots marketing campaign to bring in more new customers and establish additional returning customers. This all, in turn, helps your bottom line. And it does not need to be anything over the top. A nice thank you card or a sincere expression of gratitude is all it takes. Of course, if you can, try going beyond that with a handwritten letter or a special "gift" in the mail "just because." Request that they write a review and testimonial that you can showcase on your website. Choose a way to reward your loyal group that resonates with your brand and purpose.

This little step is so important to your strategy. Forgetting this can do some major harm to your sales and profits. In addition to fostering the positive relationships, showing that you take the time to care about your customers also does wonders for bringing in unassociated new customers. Remember, a person wants to feel like they are connected to a community, and when you make it personal and supportive, they think that your brand is the community they are looking for.

Suggestion 7: Take the Time to Compete

Competition is a great thing if you approach it as a sport rather than a personal attack. Businesses are usually not trying to sneak up on you in a dark alley to steal your wallet. Instead, think of a competitor as an opposing team, facing off from you on the field. You know what they want, and they know what you want, and you need to bring your "A" game to hold your ground with them. And as long as both of you have good sportsmanship, there is no reason you cannot pat them on the back for a good game and even a win. But just like playing sports, you can learn a lot from your opposition, even before stepping onto that field. Take the time to observe how they do business. See what they do well and what they are leaving open for you to jump in on. Use your knowledge of what they are doing to do your business better.

Think about Pizza Hut and Dominos. Two opposing pizza chains sometimes square off in media about their offerings, but you never really see them attacking one another, but rather finding new ways to attract customers and bring them to one side or the other. Just remember, you are different from the other team. You offer a purpose that is unique to your brand. If you are constantly responding to competition, you risk losing that unique spark that makes your brand special. The key here again is a balance.

The "Good" and the "Bad" and What Makes Them That Way

It is time to look more deeply at some great branding strategies and some that missed the mark to apply what you just learned. Look for what makes one effective or ineffective and why. Some brands below may not be as familiar as others, so doing a little background research into the company can help in the analysis process, but the majority should be mainstream, allowing you to rely on your knowledge of their purpose or product offering.

"Good" #1: Bank of America and Simple

Look at the difference between the two banking systems. Bank of America is the second largest bank in America while Simple is an online-only banking system that is relatively new. Notice how streamlined the website for Simple is, especially compared to Bank of America's website. There is still a place for Bank of America, as more traditional and "old school" customers valued the in-person interaction of a teller or banker, as well as options like CDs and home loans. But more contemporary customers are looking for something more tech-based and easy to use. This gave rise to Simple and the "new" way of banking.

"Good" #2: Tesla and Prius

Think about the "traditional" or "mainstream" electric cars. And think about the customers of these cars. It is safe to say, the people purchasing these cars wanted something more economical and environmentally friendly than flashy or convenient. But then Tesla joined the market and brought a luxury electric car to the customers. And it was a sports car, too! Tesla did not compete with Prius for their share of the market but rather opened up the market to new customers. A bold move but shows to be profitable. And how has that affected Prius? Are they doing it "wrong" because they continue to offer a more economical than a flashy car?

"Good" #3: JetBlue and Delta

Delta, a long time central brand in the airline business, had to start finding ways to cut down on costs and so started cutting back on your leg room and snack options. It is all business, and so are their customers. But then, JetBlue bounced into the scene with a brand strategy expressing fun and friendly. They messaged about their great snack options and roomy leg space. Delta's strategy is about efficiency and rewards for frequent flying, while JetBlue reintroduced the idea of fun in flying, despite its limited international options or less robust frequent flying program.

"Good" #4: Taco Bell and Chipotle

If you wanted cheap and fast Mexican inspired food, you went to Taco Bell. But then Chipotle came in and offered fast Mexican food with better quality, just not as cheap. Taco Bell focused on its established brand strategy, including focusing on their low price point, while Chipotle focused on a more urban message with a humorous twist. Neither is "wrong," but both compete for a share of the market in their own way, true to their deeper purpose. If you are not familiar with either brand, you should dive a little deeper into their mission and vision to uncover their purpose, and you will see just how well each strategy aligns for their brands.

"Good" #5: Dollar Shave Club and Gillette

Another great example of two brands in the same market, playing "nice" with one another and staying true to their purpose, is Dollar Shave Club and Gillette. A professional and very masculine man used Gillette razors, at least that is how the brand strategy plays out. They are a pillar of the market. But then the Dollar Shave Club joined the group, challenging the cost of a good razor. The name alone shows how aligned the company is with its brand strategy and purpose. But in addition to the price, Dollar Shave Club also looks to compete with quality. Gillette continues to focus on professional men and their needs, while Dollar Shave Club takes a more playful approach, capturing a different customer base.

"Good" #6: Whole Foods and Trader Joes

When you first look at the messaging from Whole Foods and Trader Joe's, you may think they are similar. And yes, both food stores offer a boutique grocery experience but look deeper into the two examples below and the different brands. For example, Whole Foods is a large chain with a well-off customer base. The messaging is a bit more refined and crisp. Their typography and text is cleaner, and the green color of the brand reflects the connection between nature and organic sources. Trader Joe's, on the other hand, is a smaller store. They offer more unique food options that have a little more quirk to them, just like their customers. You can see this personality appear in their name and logo as well, considering the fun typography of their name and the bright red colors of the brand. This is again another excellent example of excellent branding for two different companies with distinct missions, visions, and purpose.

"Good" #7: Uber and Lyft

Ride-sharing is a big deal in transportation these days, and Uber and Lyft are two of the big names out there. And while they both offer essentially the same service, the position of their brand is very different. Uber was the first on the scene to make a splash, placing it in the "mainstream" and "central" location of the market. The brand was sleek and modern. In fact, when the brand started, the cars were all unmarked, black Lincoln Town Cars. The feeling was luxury and modern. Now, the brand has expanded more to reach a wider customer base, now allowing cars like a Prius to pick up just about anyone, but it still retains its sleek and modern brand strategy. Lyft, on the other hand, came in with a different approach. If you were aware of Lyft, in the beginning, you might remember seeing cars driving around with a big, fuzzy pink mustache adorning their cars. The drivers were supposed to be interesting and encourage their riders to have fun, part of which included offering the front passenger seat to their riders. This is a great example of a brand entering a market with a strategy to stand apart from the already established competition. Of course, they did not "reinvent" the service they offered, essentially copying what Uber was already doing. They just took their brand in a very different direction. And it pushed Uber to become "better," as well.

But just like there are the "good," there are the "bad." What is hard from a business and marketing standpoint is that it almost always sounds great when discussing it into the bubble of meeting space. The glossy images and great backstory, as well as the ingrained brand, all blind you to the "faults" of the strategy. In 2018, for example, some of the big brands fell victim to some bad strategy. Here are a few of them for you to see and identify where in the process things "took a left turn."

. . .

"Bad" #1: H&M

At the start of the year in 2018, H&M put out a visual message on their website for little boys clothing. On one boy was a shirt with the words, "Coolest Monkey in the Jungle," and on the other, "Mangrove Jungle Survivor Expert." And while this may not sound too bad, add in the details of the image, such as the color of the skin of the two boys. One little boy appeared to be African-American, while the other appeared Caucasian. Twitter erupted when customers saw this image, questioning why the one was an animal while the other was an expert. Clearly, the cultural sensitivity of the brand was not considered when putting out this message.

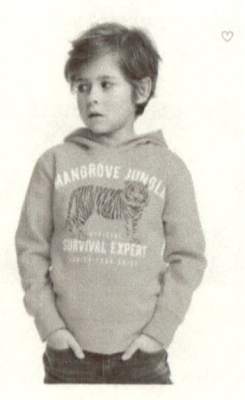

"Bad" #2: Estee Lauder

Another rollout in January of 2018 was a campaign by Estee Lauder. They debuted a line of foundation called "Double Nude Wear," which offered over 30 different shades of face coverage with SPF 25. The problem? Almost ¾ of the shades were for light skin tones. Any woman with color would have to look elsewhere for their coverage. This product development and messaging sent a very apparent message to the market that they simply do not cater to women of color, showing again, another case of cultural insensitivity.

"Bad" #3: Heineken

Another case of cultural insensitivity came in an advertisement from Heineken in March of 2018. It was a short ad, about 30 seconds long, showcasing a bartender sliding a bottle of the beer down to an attractive woman. The problem was what surrounded this action. The bartender slid the drink past several means of color, to the woman who had lighter skin. When the action was complete, the ad offered a tagline that read, "Sometimes, lighter is better." This racist messaging does not align with the brand's purpose but definitely left a "bad taste" in many people's mouth regarding the brand.

"Bad" #4: Target

When June of 2018 rolled around, people were getting ready to celebrate their fathers for Father's Day. Shoppers were pretty surprised when they went to Target to get a card and found one with an African-American couple embracing on the front and the words "Baby Daddy" scrawled across the image. And to make it worse, this was the only card option that featured an African-American family unit. Again, an example of a brand not making conscious decisions aligned with their brand strategy and being insensitive to their customer base. It did not take long for Target to pull all the cards from the shelves of their stores and issue a public apology, but the message was already out there.

"Bad" #5: Domino's Pizza

While Domino's also made the "good" list, they have had their own share of missteps. One recent misstep in 2018 was from a Russian owned franchise. To boost visibility of the brand the store created a challenge. The store offered 100 free pizzas for 100 years to anyone that tattooed the logo on their skin permanently. They soon realized that there were plenty of people willing to participate and had to place restrictions on the contest, but that was after several hundred had already gone out and inked their body with the iconic red and blue domino. And while the promotion was planned to last about 30 days, the store ended up closing the contest down after just a few days because of all the participation. Now, while this type of publicity is not really a "bad" thing, it was the lack of research and proper planning that sent this contest off course.

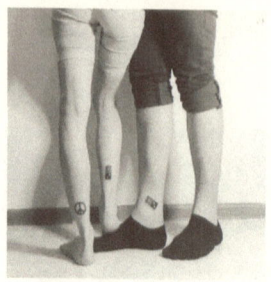

"Bad" #6: Dolce and Gabbana

Later in the year, the luxury fashion brand released a new marketing campaign that many people had a big problem with. The brand featured various ethnicities in a glaringly stereotypical situation. For example, a Chinese model was shown failing to eat Italian cuisine with chopsticks. Other than the sexual undertone, which does align with the brand's strategy, the culturally insensitive message of "unrefined Chinese people who do not understand culture" was not part of the strategy. What made it worse for the brand was a series of leaked Tweets right after this campaign. Tweets from one of the co-founders of the brand, Stefano Gabbana, exposed his opinion of the Chinese people and the country. Unfortunately for the brand, the co-founder's opinion appeared to match the message presented in their marketing campaign. As a result of this combination of "bad," Dolce and Gabbana publicly apologized and also canceled their runway show scheduled for Shanghai, ultimately costing the brand millions of dollars.

Brand Identity

3
HOW TO BEGIN TO BUILD YOUR BRAND AMONG YOUR CUSTOMERS

When you are starting up your brand, it can seem pretty exciting but a little bit overwhelming, too. When you are still a "young" brand or business owner, the best thing you can do is your research. It is valuable to talk to professionals and learn ways to succeed from those that have done it before. The purpose of this chapter is to offer a myriad of advice from different sources to help build up your brand to your customers. To begin, here are just a few general tips to understand.

1. Get some training. This does not have to cost you a fortune or require a lot of your time. There are plenty of online courses and training you can consider. Look for training on topics you do not feel confident in. This way, you can expand on your understanding of a topic with additional expertise and other people looking for support like you.
2. Change your mindset from "analysis" to "architect." After a while, all the research in the world is going to

do you no good in the success of your business. You need to do something with it. There comes a time when you need to shift from analyzing to the building. You have to put those processes into place.
3. Be acutely aware of the "no zone" for your brand. There are names, terms, and "hot buttons" that you need to avoid when developing your brand. Learn what they are and stay away from them. And off this should be done well before you start building your brand. This all depends on your company, market, and brand strategy, but it is important to know what customers are not expecting to see and what you cannot do before you throw something out to the public.
4. Try mapping out the journey of your customer. Almost all of your customers will come to engage with your brand through a series of similar steps. This "journey" is important to understand because you will then know what research the customer has probably already done or not done, and what they are searching for. This is a great way to figure out how to position your brand and offer solutions that are relevant to the place your customer is coming from.
5. Figure out how to trigger behaviors through emails. If you want to reach your customers, you need to be able to market through email. It is a "must." But you do not want to send out just any email; you want to offer content that encourages a certain behavior from your customers. This is a great way to reinforce your brand strategy and image while also increasing sales and revenue.
6. Understand social algorithms and how to maximize

your content. Think about Facebook as a great example of changing algorithms. They are always tweaking their methods for balancing business with personal. What is hard for business owners is the constant re-focus on providing a positive personal experience, making it challenging for a brand to really stand out on their site. Despite the headache of staying on top and adjusting to the changes, it is still a great place to showcase your brand, so make sure to stay on top of the changes to get the most from the free resource.

7. Automation is a good thing, even for new brands. You need to save time where you can, and finding a way to automate a process is an excellent way to start. Look for places that you can create a system of actions so you can focus your attention on other areas of your brand strategy.

8. Determine the best spot to launch your brand. Just like opening a business, location is everything. The place that you roll out your brand is powerful, and you should give it almost as much thought as the messaging you are going to present to the public. Think about a brand rollout that mirrors something that already exists in one county, but nothing exists like it in another. The response from the market will be very different, as well as your success, just by changing a zip code.

9. Another note on social media, develop a dashboard. Social media marketing is a powerful tool for your business, especially because it is free and widely used by all sorts of people. But if you want to get your brand out on multiple platforms, as you should, managing

the content for each individual site can be time-consuming. Instead, look for a dashboard that can offer some time-savings here. It may cost you something, but the rewards and time saved can be worth it.

Now that you have a good base of knowledge and some suggestions on additional areas to research more, below are specific advice on things like defining your target market and answering the needs of those customers.

Find and Reach Your Target Market

Now, more than ever, it is critical that you define your target market. It does not make financial sense to try to reach every person, especially smaller or newer brands. And if you are a small brand trying to carve out your own piece of the market among the big competitors out there, the best way to do it is with a niche market. A common mistake many brands make is focusing on "anyone willing to respond to the brand." Another is saying you want to target a group like stay at home moms or small business owners. These are good places to start, but they are so general that you will not be able to reach all the different people in those groups without focusing on a niche group of them.

By focusing on a smaller group of people in a specific market does not mean you are restricting your brand from everyone else. On the contrary, you are just focusing your attention on the part of the market that will be more likely to buy from you in the first place, but the others that become exposed to your brand can still take part in your services. This approach is simply a dollars-and-cents marketing decision focused on effective, efficient, and affordable decisions to do business. Think about an interior design business. They could say they want to market to home owner's but that, again, is far too general. Instead, they could narrow it down to homeowners living in Clearwater, Florida who make over $150,000 household income per year and are between the ages of 35 and 60. This is starting to get more specific. But to really develop a niche strategy, the business can go further by focusing on a specific area of the home to specialize in, such as bathrooms or kitchens, and style, such as mid-century modern. And of course, the age range can also be split apart, focusing on the younger end of the range as on-the-go parents or younger professionals and the latter end of the range as retirees and "empty nesters." When a company can break their target market down like this, they can customize their brand strategy to talk directly to these people instead of just speaking in general, broad-stroke terms.

To help you find and define your own target market, consider the following points:

- Look long and hard at any existing customers. Who exactly are they? What and why do they buy from you? Is there any common thread between them? What group of people are your loyal or best customers?
- Scope out the competition. Look at the type of people that your competition is talking to. And look at the customers interacting with their brand. Write down the specifics of who you think and see the focus of their attention and make sure to go a different way with your strategy. Ideally, while digging in here, you will find a niche of the market

that they are not targeting that fits in with your purpose and plans.
- Know the in's and out's of your products. Break down the features of your products. And then next to each feature, list out the pros and cons of the feature. Now, next to those benefits, write down the types of people that could use that benefit in their lives. Most likely, you will have a very general idea of your market with these answers, but it does offer a good starting point!
- Think about all the following factors for those that need your brand and those who will probably interact with it. Sometimes these are the same people, but other times, they are not. The following factors include:

- Ethnicity
- Occupation
- Family dynamic
- Education
- Income
- Gender
- Geographic location
- Age

Now do the same with the psychographics of your market. These things are a bit more personal. They are not really things you can figure out from a census or general survey. These are habits, personality traits, and more. Some of the topics you need to consider include:

- Behaviors
- Lifestyle

- Hobbies and interests
- Values
- Attitude
- Personality traits

When you come up with some things that are special to your niche, make sure you answer the following questions:

- How does your brand fit into their lifestyle?
- When will this market engage with your brand and how?
- What features align most with the psychographics of your niche?
- What media sources do these people engage with?

Watch how well your decisions perform. Once you decide what you are going to do, think about the following questions and make sure the brand strategy performs according to your expectation. The following questions to answer include:

- Does your brand reach your market easily?
- Can the niche market afford your brand?
- Have you accurately determined the driving forces behind your customer's decisions?
- Is there a real benefit to this niche and are they identifying the benefit?
- Are there enough people in this group to justify targeting them?

But now that you know what you need to do, how do you do it? Where in the world do you find this information? Well, a couple of decades ago, it would take some serious legwork.

Now, with the information overload on the Internet, you have all your answers at your fingertips. Chances are if you come up with a potential market, you can type it into Google and see what research has already been conducted on that group. You can also read articles published in newspapers, blogs, and magazines about the group you are looking into. Many times, you can find results from surveys on a specific group, but if you cannot, put together your own survey and get it out there. In addition, if you already have a customer base, ask them!

Finding the right balance for a target market is easier to do now than it was in the past, but it is still a challenge to get it right. The good news is, that once you get the group defined, getting your brand in front of them is much easier. Even coming up with messaging that reaches them is easier once you define your niche. And, of course, you get to save a lot of money only working with a small group, instead of trying to mass market to a wide range of unknown people. The return on your investment and time spent is far greater when you put in the time.

Real Steps for Responding to Customer's Needs, Even Before They Know They Need It

One of the biggest problems you may face in determining how you can communicate with your customers is that you are always focused on how products function and instead focusing on the problem that these products solve. After all, a product is just a solution to something more than it is a collection of features or a tool for your customers. Below are four tips to help you figure out what your customers are really looking for, even if they cannot identify their needs themselves.

. . .

Tip 1: Determine the problem worth solving

Sometimes, your customers simply do not have the language or vision to see the solution to their problem. This is why asking them what they want can only bring you so far. Instead, you want to figure out the true problem. This concept came about when Henry Ford created the automobile in response to his customers wanting a "faster horse." He went beyond just an incremental change to their wants, which was a faster horse, and delivered something, that answered their true need, a more convenient and effective means of transportation. A more modern example is the change from the Netflix mail delivery system of DVD to a streaming service. When they first took over the market for at-home entertainment, they offered DVD's to your doorstep by ordering them online. But if they had asked their customer's what they wanted and only answered those wants, they would have only changed the mail carrier or the selection of DVD to their customers. Instead, they recognized the true desire or problem; customers wanted faster and easier access to movies.

The better you get at figuring out the "true" problem for your customers, not just the surface ones that they articulate, the better you can tailor your brand to answer their needs. In addition, you can bring delight and unexpected joy to their lives just by predicting their needs before they even know about them!

Tip 2: Understand what customers of your customers are really wanting

This is really only relevant to your brand strategy if you are engaging business to business, but it is important to consider. You do not only want to learn what your customer's needs are but figure out what their customers ultimately want, as well.

This does require for you to look beyond the single pane of your customer and look all the way to the end result. Doing this helps you come up with solutions that your customers, and even their customers, do not even know they want yet. For example, if you offer solutions to healthcare companies, you need to look into the needs of their end customers. Could they use a solution for media presence and credibility? When you present this feature of your brand to your healthcare customers, present this solution to a problem they have not even formulated in their own strategy yet. This brings your brand beyond surface and mediocrity to distinctive and a leader in the market.

Tip 3: Do not listen to your customer anymore

Well, do not ignore them or listen to their ideas, but also do not base your decisions only on what they have to say to you. Their frame of reference is not always well-rounded. After all, they only know what they have been exposed to and used in the past. Their ideas of where you should take your business and brand are often misleading. Their feedback on how they think your current brand is working is great, but plans for your future are not best derived from them.

Think about how Hollywood produces movies today. They combine ideas that were successful last year, and they conduct focus groups and survey and test their ideas. Most of the time, there are multiple endings written and filmed just so they can test out which one resonates best with a general audience. This explains why "blockbusters" are so predictable and familiar. It is why you can pretty much guess the ending within the first few minutes of the film. It is a safe approach to get their return on their big investment, instead of trying to break the mold and deliver something viewers did not even know they wanted to engage with.

Now think about the Sundance Film Festival in Park City, Utah. Small producers and directors show their work to festival-goers, not afraid to take the risk because the budget is reasonable and expectations are level. This is why new concepts find their way onto your movie or television screen. Think of films like the Blair Witch Project and how on a "shoestring" budget of only a few thousand dollars they were able to give an audience something new and unexpected, generating over a $100 million in revenue. Part of this success can be attributed to not listening to what their customers wanted. They delivered what they discovered was the true "need" of their viewers. If all brands listened too closely to their customers, the world probably would not have things like Mac computers or iPhones.

Tip 4: Get to know the lives and jobs of your niche target market intimately

The reason this is so important for you to know goes back to the first part of this section. Your brand needs to respond to customers' true needs or answer their real problems, not just present them with features or offer a tool for their lives. You do not want to try to force your brand on them, but rather guide them to see how it fits seamlessly into their lives. The best way to do this is to know a lot about their lives. For example, if you only asked your customers what they wanted in a new lawnmower, your product would reflect the interest in a quieter motor or bigger bag for catching grass. These improvements are good, but when you recognize that the majority of the people to which you market are homeowners living in southern states, such as Georgia and Florida, you can recognize that cutting grass in the humidity and heat can be uncomfortable at best but dangerous to their health on the other end. Understanding this, you can offer an add-on or feature that addresses the issue of heat.

When you expand your understanding to who your customers really are and how they interact with your brand, you can use that information to better tailor your brand strategy. When you do this, you can offer a message and image to your customers that show them you understand what they are going through and are active in offering solutions for their lives. Actions like this set you apart and build loyalty easily.

How to Survey and Respond to Some of the Most Common Needs

When you want to be inspired, do you act like many other companies and look to the new products being released, the trendy topics in your market, or even competing companies that appear to be doing well? This is not wrong or bad, but it is not the only place to go to keep your brand relevant in your market. Your customer's response and interests are there, in your face, waiting to give you the answers you need to be "on it." After all, it is your customers that determine how your company progresses and its lifespan. As you create your brand experience, you need to start with your customer in mind every time.

Of course, focusing on your customer as a brand is nothing new, but many brands still struggle with how to do it exactly. If you have not centered your approach on your customer before, the task can be intimidating and the curve to learn how to do it can be steep. Like mentioned earlier, you need to be able to figure out exactly what your customers need and how you can alter your strategy to meet those needs. You can also use this information to find out what other areas of your business can change to meet the customer more fully. The guide below is designed to give you an introduction to focusing on your customers and dissect the typical roadblocks preventing brands from responding to those needs.

Before you begin, however, you need to know exactly what a "customer need" is in this context. "Need," in the context of this text, is the motivation that encourages a customer to purchase a specific brand over the other options. "Need" drives purchasing decision. To reiterate the primary motivation, brands often respond by offering a "solution" to their need or more value to the customer. How you feel at lunchtime is a good example. When you start to feel hungry, you are experiencing a need. When you start thinking about where you are going to purchase food, you are considering factors like service time, location, and a food type. Finally, where you decide to eat is ultimately your purchasing decision.

There are common classifications for the needs of customers. The top 15 include:

1. Experience: A customer should have an easy time interacting with your brand, or the way to engage with it should be very transparent. The less work they have to do to engage with your brand, the better.
2. Convenience: Your brand should clearly state how it provides a functional solution to a problem. If a problem is something your customer has yet to identify, you also need to show them why it is an issue and how your brand fills the need for a solution.
3. Price: Every person and target customer base has a

budget they operate from. Make sure you settle your brand where it makes the most sense.
4. Function: Your brand needs to mirror the function of the product. Customers should expect certain functionality and be pleased with the real functionality when they engage with a product.
5. Compatibility: The other items your customer uses need to fit with the products relevant to your brand strategy.
6. Efficient: Streamlining is heaven to a customer, so make sure to save them time with an efficient answer.
7. Performance: If you put out a message that a product performs a certain way, it needs to live up to that expectation when the customer engages with it. This is very similar to functionality.
8. Reliable: And more than just performing once the way it was expected, it should perform the same way over and over again.
9. Design: Sleek design is always attractive. But more than just looking good, your brand should also show how intuitive and easy a product is as well.

Needs specific to service includes:

1. Control: A customer wants to be in the driver seat during a transaction. In addition, a customer should still feel empowered after, if they need to make a return, change, or adjustment.
2. Transparent: Your brand needs to be clear to your customers; it is something that is expected. This means being honest about pricing, outages, and more. This transparency garners trust.

3. Fair: A brand needs to be fair to their customers. This means offering something that is good for them and good for you, including the length of contracts, service terms, and pricing.
4. Empathy: All people want to be heard, especially if they invested money into something. If a customer takes the time to contact a company, they just want a little understanding of their struggle on the other end of the phone.
5. Information: Giving details about your brand to customers starts during the investigation and research phase and continues to be important for months after the interaction. Offering "educational" tools to your customers in the form of blogs or videos is a way to help customers feel supported in their ownership of a product.
6. Options: Customers like to have purchasing options, especially within a company. This can mean a variety of payment options or product features. It provides a way for customers to personalize their experience with your brand, but also find a solution for their budget.

Now that you know the needs of customers, consider how to gain and keep a strong customer base. Part of this is doing an analysis of the needs of your customers. They will probably fall somewhere within the 15 mentioned earlier, but others could also arise. You can gather this information through surveys, as well as research more to fully understand your target niche audience.

But once you know their needs, you need to take that information and form it into a solution. To do this, you need to see the problem like you are the customer. As a customer, you would expect:

- A solution for the "real" problem.
- A nurtured relationship.
- Feedback requested.
- Instructions clear and available, so implementation is easy.
- Messaging is consistent across the brand.

4

KEEPING THE CUSTOMER ON THE HOOK

The idea of a customer "lifecycle" was developed with the concept of managing customers and their relationship with your brand, or CRM. This practice mapped the stages of a customer from the moment they consider a brand to even after they make a purchase. It is important to know the stages your customers go through before they make a purchase so you can offer the best experience and engagement possible. Another related term that is important is the lifetime value of a customer or CLV. This predictor illustrates the net profit you can expect from the total lifespan of the customer. This term also comes from the CRM practice as well as database marketing. If your brand is very customer focused, this is an important term to attach to, mainly because it is closely linked to the relationship with the customer for a long time.

When you combine the two terms, "lifecycle" and "lifetime value," you can find some incredible benefits for your brand, including things like prioritization, segmentation, and even budgeting. In some markets, the two together are also good predictors for assessing the brand's "health" as well as a guide for how to improve it. With the amount of information that these two together can tell, it should not be a surprise that many executives put it on the agenda time and time again. Finally, the two together also impact the return on marketing investments in a big way.

To dive a little deeper into the two terms, it is important first to recognize the stages of a customer lifecycle. Of course, there are many different theories and ways to define the stages, but the reality remains that it is a cycle. Customers all go through a certain loop, as long as the circle is not broken. A somewhat "traditional" loop contains the following stages:

1. Awareness
2. Knowledge
3. Consideration
4. Selection
5. Purchase
6. Satisfaction
7. Loyalty
8. Advocacy
9. Return to step 1

Another more simplified cycle shows the lifecycle as:

1. Reach - attract customers to your brand
2. Acquisition - bring the person further into the influence of the brand
3. Conversion - establish a relationship to result in a purchase

4. Retention - keep and up-sell or cross-sell to the customers deciding to make a purchase
5. Loyalty - become more of an advocate for the brand than just
6. Return to step 1

Neither of these definitions are wrong. It just is a matter of preference and relevance to your specific brand. Side note on working with influencers: do not just go for the flashy, "big" names on social media sites for advocates and influencer promotion of your brand. Often, the best influencer is the person standing in front of you making a purchase already. This also includes your employees. Do not discount the power of a happy customer, even if they do not have a widespread social media presence.

But another facet to consider when thinking about the conversion of a customer is the complex reality that this person operates in. A model or cycle is just a template; the real engagement is much more complex. No matter how it shakes out, the path that a customer takes to make a purchase and remain a customer is never a straight line or funnel down nicely into your brand. Now, more than ever, your customers are enjoying a sense of power and an array of choice. This is fueled by the proliferation of social media and the Internet.

You will never really know the journey of your customer. Maybe they saw that new billboard along the side of the highway, or maybe it was their neighbor that mentioned your brand to them over the fence this morning. You also do not really know if they engaged in any offline marketing or if it was only online and to what extent. This problem is really only the "tip of the ice burg." How many times have you identified a process or system that seemed to operate in a silo? Or maybe you noticed two systems are disjointed and disconnected? Have you noticed that now there are additional methods for interaction that these disconnects are gaping wider?

And beyond this, dive into your true understanding of your existing customers. Do you really know them well? Is there buying opportunity in some of your smaller accounts but you have not worked them efficiently? Did a customer have a strong loyalty opportunity, but you have not seen them since their first interaction with your brand? While you may be disconnected, the lifecycle is not. Your customers still go through the same cycle that they have pretty much always been through; it is just how you engage at each level of the lifecycle that has changed. Changes to the connectivity of the world have opened up a new world of opportunity for brands and customers alike, but it has also opened up new challenges as well.

But this does not only apply to the lifecycle of a customer, but it also impacts the lifetime value of them as well. Regardless of the definitions, it is still critical to align with the dimensions of the brand by matching the stages of the lifecycle with the needs, signals, and intent. The way to view customers is as a connection between all areas of your business, including your brand strategy, channels, and marketing tactics. Despite this common understanding, many tools still exist to deliver results in a very disconnected manner, often focusing on the business instead of the customer.

Looking into the lifecycle in general, there are obvious fibers that span across stages and layers. For example, some forms of marketing satisfy both the customer's intent and need, such as content marketing. But then the idea of content spans past these two stages, as it can settle into a lifecycle at other stages, such as advocacy. Social Media marketing is another example of an approach that threads through multiple stages of the customer lifecycle. Email marketing and other "traditional" marketing can also thread through stages in different ways. You are probably thinking of many other ideas in this instance; the forms your brand takes can cross multiple lines. It is important for you first to identify the "touch points" and move to the channels and tactics next. This way, you can integrate your views to draw together the goals of your business, the journey of a customer on a buying path, the cycle of sales, the experience for the customer, the channels, messaging, and, of course, the customer.

Looking More into the CLV or Lifetime Value of a Customer

Many brands often wonder how to calculate the financial value of their customers; meaning how much income can you expect from a customer? If you calculate this properly, you can determine how much you are willing to spend on a customer through actions like promotion and customer service, so you can still make a profit from the customer. As a very simplified and hypothetical example, if a CLV is $10, and you spend $8 in investing into the customer (converting and retaining them), you can expect to make $2 in profit from this customer. This method of forecasting is all about using the present to predict the future. CLV is the current financial value of your customers that you can expect in the future. But this is very macro, and to adopt this approach to a more micro action, like to brand strategy, it is difficult. Additionally, the model responds to direct marketing tactics, not for more indirect approaches, like branding.

This means you need a different method for calculating your CLV at a more micro level. One idea is for you to look directly into the return on your investment in marketing or branding activities. The basis of this approach is to look at the extra dollars expended on activities to target customers. This approach is best to figure out the lifespan and efficiency of a strategy from a financial perspective. But to do this, it is imperative you have a strong program in place to view the bottom-up lifecycle of a customer. Most companies do not have a well-rounded program, and nor do they have the means to apply it across different levels. This is just a brief explanation of another approach that still has its own challenges.

A third approach is to use your customer management system to predict the CLV. This approach can be applied globally as well as at a micro level, but it also has its own challenges. The fourth idea is to look into the equity of a customer. This approach is like combining the classical form of calculating CLV as well as the return on your marketing investment. To begin, you need to look at the total sum of customer life within the company. Using this information, you can then develop a scaffolding to enhance the lifetime value of each relationship you have with a customer from the perspective of CRM or customer relationship management. Three primary foundational considerations determine the equity of a customer:

1. The equity of value, or the view of a customer in regard to the brand from a very realistic perspective.
2. The equity of the brand.
3. The equity of retaining the customer, or developing customer loyalty.

These three "drivers" have important pieces that flex and combine to improve the financial value of the equity for a customer. As an example, if you work on the equity of value, you can offer more to your customers or make the integration or adaptation more streamlined. This action has the potential to increase the overall equity of the customer.

As you dig further into this methodology, you can play with predictive analysis for things like segmentation of your customers, and the likelihood of the customer to switch brands over time. If you begin to play around with these topics, make sure you keep a long-term perspective when applying this information to your strategy.

The attraction to this model is that it is both customers focused as well as future-oriented. Look, for example, at the three considerations listed earlier; equity of value, brand, and retention. Your brand, especially, is part of making up the value of your customer, not the other way around. This is a clear example of how this approach is focused on the customer. In addition, this approach also considers the return on your marketing investment and the obvious importance of segmentation of your customers. You'll want to see the breakdown of the return on your marketing investment by using customer equity. The following outline should assist you in visualizing the process:

Start: You Invest in Marketing

Path A:

- Cost of Marketing Investment

Path B:

- You make improvements to the three different drivers
- The customer's perceptions of your brand improve
- You increase customer attention and retention
- Overall CLV increases
- Overall equity of your customer increases

Result: You Realize Your Return on the Marketing Investment

The Alchemy of Retail: Turning Browsers into Buyers

Think about a time that you yourself went online to buy something and ended up surfing around, putting things into your virtual shopping baskets, but then never bought something, or just abandoned the basket to continue your search. As you may or may not already know, this is a very common behavior. Now, some brands are better than others at converting these browsers into buyers, but there is still opportunity left on the table for them, and you, to capitalize on this opportunity. A recent estimate shows that almost 90% of brands with an online presence do not have a strategy to re-engage browsers that abandoned their carts. Business to business customers have had strong recovery plans for browsers in the past, but now it is important for a business to consumer brands to think about this step in the process, too.

Before business to consumer or B2C, brands had a strong focus on finding new customers and re-engaging them after they reached the end of the sales cycle, but less focus was given to the potential customer that has engaged with the brand but did not end up following through on a purchase. Thankfully, the emergence of newer tech has made nurturing customers through the entire lifecycle. This also means that you can re-engage browsers after they abandon a cart or start to falter once towards the purchase. But what are effective ways to strategize methods to turn a browser into a buyer? Below are some suggestions:

Use your data to your advantage

The reason a person comes to a website can vary from person to person. Sometimes, they are there looking to make a purchase, while other times, they are simply "window shopping," or are comparing prices and brands. To better analyze your website traffic, a platform designed for commerce marketing with built-in "intelligence" provides the opportunity for you to review the data at scale. This resource helps you grasp your customer's behavior better and also give you tools to provide relevant messages for helping to recover browsers. These messages can now be personal and targeted. A dialogue about browsing habits, instead of just a generic message about a product they were looking at, is more powerful.

For example, instead of just sending a message like, "Still looking for cutting boards? Check out ...," consider a dialogue like, "looks like you are looking for new cutting boards. Check out this post about cutting board considerations! Also, here are some related products to consider (cutting board cleaner, knives, etc.)" Add links to bring them back to your site, and potentially back to the products they were looking at in the first place.

If the customer had shopped your brand previously and later abandoned a cart or was just browsing, you can use the combination of the two points of data to make your conversation even more specific. This can also be very advantageous when you are including information about a sale coming up. All of this data can provide relevant messaging, making the dialogue more impactful and beneficial to you and the customer.

Do not be a "one trick pony;" Find Multiple TouchPoints

One message is sometimes not enough to re-engage a browser. Think about sending a message to the browser at least one day after they initially abandoned their search, and then another two days after that, and another one five days after that second message. You could even add a fourth message at the one-week mark. In addition to frequency, you could also look to combine approaches with a variety of triggers and messages. For example, maybe the first message includes information just about their initial product of interest, the second could include related products to that category, and the subsequent could then include an offer or details about an upcoming sale that they can take advantage of for their purchase. No matter the messaging, it is critical to get your brand and specific products in front of them as often as possible. Thankfully, now you can do this in a dynamic manner with only minor alterations to the creative content.

Get to know your customer

Cookies are a great resource to gather different information about a customer, even if they do not have an account for your site. For instance, a single cookie can identify the path the customer took to get to your website, such as through an email. Another cookie can show you that they spent a certain amount of time on the site but left without making a purchase. Remember, your customers are probably interacting with your brand for multiple devices, as well. Many people use their phones, tablets, and computers to look for information. This means you need to be able to track across devices so that you can see a user session that begins in on one device and picks up on another. Again, using a cookie is a great way to track this. If you can get the customer to create an account for your site, you can attach a cookie that has no expiration date, so each time they "log in" to your site, you can see their activity, regardless of their device. This attachment can offer a holistic view of this particular customer's path to your brand as well as their behavior.

Once you gather this type of information from cookies, you can archive the historical data of a customer to understand better who they are and what their habits are. Then you can use this information to better target your messaging. And the more the customer engages with your brand, like signing up for emails or joining a private online community through your site, you can gather more information and provide more customized content. For example, you can send a birthday note or e-vite for an upcoming event.

Keep it personal

The message you send to your customer needs to be valuable and relevant to them. This is the only way to successfully recover them as a browser. Now, customers expect personalization. This means no matter how you communicate with them, it needs to show that you understand who they are, that you value them as a customer, and that you treat them as a unique part of your brand story. There is a fine line, however, between being encouraging and spamming. Make sure the information you send is targeted but not overly invasive. Find the balance.

In addition, make sure your data is connected so that your browsers do not get a targeted email for every single item they look at or every time they visit your site. Also, make sure that data sync to show that an item was purchased, so they do not get a message to buy after the transaction was completed. If you do not connect your data, you risk losing your customer to a competitor who has figured this step out. At the very least, you will have failed at recovering a browser.

To succeed in communicating with your customers and turning browsers into buyers, you need not only to see and learn about your customers, but you need to show them that you are doing that, too. If you are not stressing the importance of converting someone "just looking" into a customer, you should reconsider your strategy and start doing it now. It is an easy thing to start doing and can be a great place to learn more about who is interacting with your brand as well as increase sales.

How to Age Well - Tips on How to Keep Your Brand Relevant When it is No Longer New

Let us be real here for a second. It is no easy feat to keep up with the changing influences and technology. Anything you do that the public sees can dramatically shift the perception and reputation of your brand. And it can be as simple as an ill-timed or phrased tweet or post. How customers perceive their connection to your brand, if you meet their expectation of keeping up with the latest technology or products, and how you interact with your customers are all things that shape the reputation of your brand. Trying to manage your brand without considering your customers is like driving a car blindfolded, you will most certainly do some damage, which can be devastating or only minor, but you have no way to tell until it happens. You could easily drive your brand off the cliff and into the abyss if you are not careful.

The relevant brands you need to mirror also happen to be the most successful. This should not be a surprise. Think about Apple and Nike as examples. They stay on top because they are not afraid to be different. They do not play it safe and just repeat what worked in the past. And this includes the products they offer as well as how they engage and interact with their customers. The anticipation for the needs of their customers and the hawk-eye trained on the market is how these top brands keep evolving successfully.

To dig a little deeper, here is an example of how these two brands show they applied their understanding of their customers, and the market. Nike and Apple's reputation was built from various touch points. First, look at how Nike was able to bring skateboarders, who are notorious for shirking anything "corporate," into their loyal following. And not only that, Nike was able to make them a proud group of users. To do this, Nike developed its own sub-brand for just skateboarders and then brought on professional and respected skateboarders into their company to represent and develop the sub-brand, called Nike SB. The professional skateboarding athletes on the team of Nike SB and the skateboarders that were willing to consider Nike provided valuable input into what they were looking for in their gear. Nike in turn delivered on those expectations and more.

Apple's reputation is one of forward-thinking and needs anticipation. There have been some flaws in their delivery of features, but even with the mistakes, Apple continues to have a loyal following. Part of this is to do with the marketing that is always on-trend, the package design is super-modern, and their retail experiences are always engaging and contemporary. By offering an experience that is innovative in almost all areas,

Apple can afford a misstep here or there because they foster a strong reputation and customer experience. And they are almost always relevant.

As a brand moves into a more mature age, you have more data and information to work with to refine and deliver the best to your customers. With this wealth of information about customer's needs and a continued focus on innovative delivery that is beyond expectation will help you stay relevant and memorable through the years.

Four additional tips on how to keep your brand relevant as it matures include:

1. Keep communication open and flowing between you and your customers all the time. You cannot always think for your customers. You need to talk to them to solve their problems. You may be nailing it right now, but their needs may change in the future, and you should be ready to be their "hero" with a solution handy when they do. You can communicate with them by offering meeting times or focus groups to hear their ideas and needs and also what they hear "on the streets." You can use social media to poll across markets to get a wider opinion on topics. This also shows customers publicly that you care about their needs and shows your competitors that you are actively engaging your customers. You can in turn use this information to tailor your services to the real needs of your customers as well as illustrate your involvement of your customers in your decision-making process (a great value-adding feature you can promote)!

2. Look at a customer's total experience with your brand. Make sure your "story" shines in all areas of what you do, including all the channels you communicate through. This means the voice and tone of your messages should be consistent. Your graphics should be similar every time in terms of style, color, font, etc. Colors, in general, should be cohesive. The more consistent you are for the total experience, the easier it is to recognize your brand quickly. This also helps customers feel comfortable and like they "know" your brand. From this position, your customers are more likely to share your brand with others.
3. Take a little risk, be a little daring. It is not bad for you to try new things. In fact, think back to the examples of Apple and Nike. Both are successful because they take risks. This is the very foundation of how you stay relevant as you mature. It is critical that you shift your approach and change with the tides to stay relevant.
4. Always think first for the customer. This is an old tip, but it has never gone out of style. Customer-centered is vital to your continued success. This should be obvious just thinking about the first tip of this list, communicate with your customers. Deliver solutions to their current needs and for anticipated needs, even before they can form the need in their mind.

In general, make sure your customers trust your brand. Trust leads to loyalty, which leads to word-of-mouth marketing from your loyal customers, which leads to increased revenue and continued success.

5
SEALING THE DEAL

Congratulations! You just developed the most amazing direct mail items ever created. Or, your newest magazine should have its own shelf space in the Guggenheim. And, your snazzy brochure is being replicated by the competition because there is nothing better. Your online presence and campaign made the inventors of the Internet, Vint Cerf and Robert Kahn, tip their hats to you. But the sales just are not there on the other side of all of this effort.

Assume that you know the marketing channels are appropriate and your product is top notch, there are still a few things that could be going on that is stopping you from getting the sales you are working for. With these assumptions in place, you need to look long and hard at your messaging going out, especially at your call to action. As in any strategy for marketing, you must motivate your customers to make a decision swiftly. Most of the time, when they are faltering between "just looking" and handing over their payment, it is a simple case of restructuring your motivating comments. Some of the best ways to motivate your customers include:

1. Set the deadline. The order must be placed by a certain day and time to qualify for the deal. This could mean a special discount or a free gift or an upgrade to your purchase. For example, "Shop now! Sale ends on 1/10/19 at 11:59 PM EST!"
2. And set the deadline month in conjunction with the month they will receive their product. Let your customers know that if they purchase before the deadline, they will get it by a certain date so they will be motivated to make a decision right then, even if your competition is offering a similar product.
3. Let customers know when prices will go up. A good deal is attractive to every person, no matter his or her financial status. If you know that you will be raising your prices on a specific date, let your customers know, too. This way they know that they need to make their purchase before that date to take advantage of the lower costs. For example, if you offer a membership service, like Amazon's Prime membership, and the price will go up on the first of the year, let your customers know and watch how the membership will spike right before!
4. Offer a period for customers to try out or become introduced to your brand with less risk. New customers love the idea of trying something out before committing to it. During the trial period, provide your customers with a low price, additional services, or a special deal. But, on the other hand, when it is time to cancel the membership, do not make it hard. You want

people to walk away with a "good taste in their mouth" regarding their interaction with your brand, even if they did not stay a customer.
5. Give away a "free" gift with their purchase. Anytime you can provide something "free" to your customer, you are almost guaranteed to increase sales. Like the third tip, every person appreciates a good deal. To add extra motivation for buying and getting the gift, consider offering this deal to the first 25, 50, or 100 people who reply to the offer.
6. Offer a trial period that is "no risk" or "risk-free." The terms in this tip are vital to the success of the trial. When there is no risk of taking action, people are more likely to move forward with a decision. If a customer finds that they do not like the product or service in any way, they feel confident that they can cancel within the trial period time and not risk a thing.
7. Be clear about if something is only available in-store or online. This honest marketing message helps your customers recognize that they need to make a decision in one place, encouraging them to not "shop around" online and in store for the product or service.
8. Allow customers an upgrade for free. For example, "Make a purchase in the next four days and your product will be upgraded to the next model up." This is a great offer for someone who wants the "better" or more advanced option but is choosing their selection because of the price. It also reinforces the concept of getting a good deal. Contrary to what you may think, the increase in sales often makes up for the loss in profits.
9. Offer complimentary accessories or supplies with a

purchase. Computers are notorious for making an offer like this. If you purchase the computer, you get a free carrying case, wireless mouse, or printer. Or, if you purchase a printer, you get extra ink and printer paper. Almost any product can have complimentary accessories or supplies attached to it. Of course, make sure to have a deadline for this type of offer. This way people know they need to act on this offer before it expires.

10. Encourage customers to tell their friends about your brand. This is especially great for brands that operate within the service industry. For example, if a customer tells a friend to try out their gym, they in return get a free t-shirt or personal training session.
11. Use your words carefully, making sure they encourage action and are powerful. Phrases that are action-oriented are powerful. Consider phrases such as the following:

- Only 5 left!
- Chat live now.
- Contact us now for more details.
- Use the pre-paid envelope to mail in your coupon today.
- Available 24-hours a day, 7-days a week.
- Call/act now!

It would be a great universe if a potential customer became a loyal customer after they engage in your brand the first time, silently paying the full asking price for whatever you put in front of them. The reality is that almost any sale is not this easy. And sometimes it can seem like no matter what you do, this one customer just keeps making things harder than necessary and appears impossible to win over. A deal can sometimes drag on for weeks and weeks if you engage with a customer who fears to take the next step or wants to push back on you. And if you find yourself in this situation, there is a strong chance that the exchange will not end in your favor.

One of the most important things you can control in a situation like this is how you respond to the customer. Do not fool yourself into thinking you can control their attitude. And even if this is the worst customer in the world, you can take certain steps to improve the odds of making the sale. Below are nine tips for engaging with a tough customer. This includes difficult people, someone who does not want to commit, and even bullies.

Tip 1: Do not show them you are anxious or reacting to their behavior

A bully is more likely to try to push you if they sense you are nervous or afraid. Try not to speed up the conversation or change how you respond when in an interaction with someone who is challenging. On the other hand, you should stay on task. Do not speed up something that needs time or shortens the process if they are acting flustered. Follow your protocols, no matter the person.

Tip 2: Be firm in your resolve

It can be easy to become frustrated when a customer is pushing on you about something, but the frustration is only going to get in the way of the sale. The person engaging with you may be noncommittal or even a bully, but they could still desire whatever it is that you are selling. This means you need to stand your ground and keep to your normal approach to closing a sale. Do not let your emotions run away with you.

Tip 3: Mirror the response of the customer, if appropriate

Matching the behavior of a bully is sometimes the most effective method for getting them to calm down. This can mean mirroring their tone, strength, or pace. When you rise to their response style, you may be just aggressive enough to make them back off. In addition, a strong person challenging you often respects strong people in return. Showing them that you are able to rise to the occasion can grab their attention and win their admiration.

Tip 4: Ask for them to explain their challenges more

A person who is giving you a hard time is often giving others a hard time, and it all probably stems from the millions of things bogging down on their mind. Most of the time, they are just not willing to listen to you because it would just add to the swirling thoughts in their brain already. Instead of trying to force them to listen, try to get them talking, especially about their challenges. Taking this approach helps you break down the animosity and opens up their emotions to you. This is a great tactic for those that do not want to commit to the purchase. When you figure out the problems of this customer, you can use this information to determine if solving their problems is really worth it.

Tip 5: Uncover the top priorities for the customer in this situation

Find out the short-term goals that are a priority for your customer. A great phrase to ask them includes, "What are the more pressing priorities you want to see accomplished in the next year?" This objective can be the central point for your solution, and you can instill a sense of urgency for even those that are most fearful of a commitment.

Tip 6: Work on establishing a realistic buy-in

Use the information the customer has shared with you during the conversation to determine their seriousness in solving their problems. Do this before you even start your proposal or sales pitch. Do not just ask if they are committed to buying from you, but rather, ask them if they are committed to doing something immediately. This soft commitment to action gently holds their "feet to the fire" and can help you gauge their level of commitment when it comes time to ask them to purchase.

Tip 7: Control the conversation casually

Hijacking the conversation is a real challenge when working with a difficult person. Sometimes this means a person goes off on an unrelated tangent or they move the direction of the conversation in different directions. Other times they could simply try to talk over you. Selling requires you always to control the conversation. If you recognize that the conversation is not going in the best direction, you can interrupt the customer by saying something like, "Pardon me, I would love to talk about this more after this meeting, but to respect the time of all parties, it is important to stay on track and on agenda." Using a strong and directive phrase like this can help keep the conversation going in line with the needs of the customer.

Tip 8: Do not exert or try to establish dominance in the conversation

Dominance is exerted in conversation with phrases like, "no offense," "actually," and "did you know...." If you are working with a hard customer, these missteps will not develop the power you were hoping to achieve. Of course, you want to appear as an authority, particularly when talking with a challenging customer, but the best way to do this is by offering objective information and requesting the customer share their perspectives with you. To illustrate the different approach, consider the statement, "Did you know that over the next six years, production is expected to double in size, according to the Wall Street Journal?" This is a clear statement of dominance. Instead, consider saying, "I heard that production is expected to double over the next six years. Do you anticipate this to impact your business?" This rephrasing of the same information shows the customer that you know your facts and want their input.

Tip 9: Keep in mind, this is not personal

Unfortunately, challenging customers are just a part of a business. They are a constant element of the sales cycle. Because this is something that continues to happen over and over, you need to remember that you do not need to take it seriously. You can always leave the meeting or discussion if things get out of hand, but always remember to be respectful. The behavior of the customer is not a reflection of who you are. Most likely, it is simply the response to the customer's own issues that you cannot solve. Leave the interaction, go home, eat a good meal, talk with friends about something that is important, and find a way to let it go so you can go back in the next day ready to move forward. It is not fun dealing with hard customers, but dealing with them in the "right" way can still yield profits. Come up with a game plan that works for you so you do not buckle under their pressure and so you do not take their behavior personally.

Strengthen Your Brand

Walter Landor, a pioneer in branding, said, "Products are made in a factory, but brands are made in the mind." The value of your customers is different from the physical cost of producing that product. Your brand value is what matters in the marketplace, and it all comes from how your customers perceive you. This means that you can build up your value and share the message of this value to customers, helping your brand succeed for a long time.

How your customers perceive your services and products is called "brand equity." Consider brands that you know of that probably have high brand equity. Did industry-leaders like Microsoft, Google, or Apple come to mind? These are all great examples of high brand equity.

While your brand is a challenge to speak of in terms of dollar amount, you know that when your brand is strong, your bottom line improves. This is because your brand strength directly impacts customer satisfaction, your reputation in the market, your credibility as a leader, and awareness of your brand in general. The impact in these four areas is especially helpful because marketers can use these as resources for bringing in customers that are attracted to brands with a lot of value.

A customer can come to your brand by mistake and not really have a background of research, or they can be "mindful," and come in with strong intention. Now that the recession is on the decline, and the economy is moving back to balance, customers are becoming more "mindful," or intentional. This translates to a consumer who will spend money on something that they feel is a good value. Some of the considerations of this customer include:

- Understanding their options, for both products and brands. Almost 70% of a customer's lifecycle takes place online, meaning that they know what is being offered, what the best features are, the best price, and reputable brands selling it. By the time you get to meet them, they have done their research.
- They also read reviews and talk to people about their needs. Especially if you are promoting something necessary, valuable, or expensive, your customers are going to find out how the other people who have engaged with your brand liked their experience. This means that they read reviews left by your customers on various platforms, check social media to find out who has experience with the brand or product, and talk with their circle of influence about their ideas. They are making sure that you are not the only person that thinks your product is the best on the market.
- A link between their selection and their identity. There is a relationship between their purchase and who they are. They have their own "personal brand," even if they do not recognize it. They are going to select brands and products that mirror or accent their own brand.

All of these considerations impact the decision a customer makes, and it goes far beyond the features of the product you are promoting. Stripping away all the details from a customer's sales process, the heart of it rests in the "bond" they want to create with a brand that they perceive as having high equity.

But you cannot just tell a customer that you are valuable. You need to show them through your brand messaging. Again, a brand is "created in the mind." Use this foundational understanding to build your value from there. Below are some suggestions on how to do this:

- Start from inside your brand and move out from there.

There is so much for your customers to look at that if your product does not have something worth noticing built into it, it is going to get skipped over. You need to stand out from a product and brand level. Think of this in terms of superlatives. You are top in customer service in your market. You win the award for the most satisfied employees or can celebrate your new "Most Innovative" award for your brand. Branding goes beyond just marketing. It extends into every part of a business. This is a great method for showing value at all levels. This is what makes the customer experience great.

- Make sure your message for your brand is targeted.

If you want to get your message out, find the group of people that are dying to hear what you want to say. You are not throwing out a generic message, hoping to hit a few people that would want your product, but rather are communicating with the people that would find your brand valuable already. To do this, you need to make sure your channels for marketing are ideal and that your message is tailored to those channels. For example, consider the advertisements from Adidas and Nike during the 2014 World Cup. Adidas provided a good message about "winning or losing," but Nike stole the show with strong and targeted messaging, clearly made for only those who followed football closely. Their message was limited to the direct audience, and that was what built value, which Adidas ended up missing out on.

- Your design needs to stay strong.

The way you showcase your brand is very visual. It includes the design elements, font, shape, and color of your brand. It is applied to places like your website, email messages, packaging, and more. The way you use these elements is the non-verbal way to communicate your value to your customers. If you are a small company, a good system for branding can make you seem powerful. Or if you are a large company, good branding can enhance your strength in the market. But bad design can do the exact opposite.

- Have meaning behind your brand choices.

Value is a perception by your customers. Think of the phrase, "beauty is in the eye of the beholder." The same theory applies to brand value. To help inject meaning behind your brand choices, consider the following:

- Create the perception of your brand as a symbol of status. Make it important enough to protect or guard, even if you do not change the product itself.
- Become a symbol. Think about Toms shoes as an example. Customers knew that when they purchased a pair of their shoes, a pair was being donated to a child in need. This symbol drove customers to purchase this brand over competitors who did not promote this benefit.
- Make it emotional. If you have a product that is similar to your competition, then you need to rely on the emotional connection to your brand. Remember, customers want to feel connected, so if they feel they

are linked to your brand and you always deliver on and beyond their expectations, you are building loyalty. To do this, present your product with empathy, no matter what it is.
- Offer content that is valuable. Being a thought leader and offering it to your customers for free is important in building trust. It can also be entertaining and just enough to turn a customer who only purchased once into a loyal customer. They can even become brand advocates. The trick to this is developing content that increases value for your brand and also offers value for your customers. Some tips on how to do this include:

1. Develop a persona for your buyer and speak to them. A persona includes demographic details such as age and occupation, as well as psychographic information like interests and problems.
2. Develop stories about your customers. Make content that reflects the customer engaging with it, not your goals for your marketing strategy. You want your customers to discover your brand's value, not try to force them to read your opinion of it.
3. Keep it simple and clear. Choose language that is plain and accessible. Your "business talk" is fine in your office, but when communicating with the public, leave the acronyms and monikers at the office. Speak to the customer, not to your associates.

- Create a loyal following.

The relationship you are developing with your customers is meant to be long-term, so make sure to start that relationship with content that is tailored to them. The more you put out content that aligns with their interests and needs, the more often they will come back to you for information. You can do this by using certain platforms, like social media or email, to give different types of messaging. Social is a great place for humor and enjoyment. Email can be more specific to a single product or product line that they showed interest in already. Tailoring an email with a more personalized approach is valuable to customers, while a more generic message on social media is expected.

After everything is cleared away, it should be clear to you that your customers are your best support for the strength of your brand. You need social proof in the form of reviews and recommendations to help win more customers, but these things come from customers, meaning you need to get a group of customers to be loyal to your brand to start this strengthening process.

Part of that process is making your brand distinct in the marketplace. You need to stand apart from the competition. Your brand's story needs to be better than the others for the customer base you are targeting. In addition, your story needs to be consistent. But, as with anything in life, it needs to change with the market. It requires you to adapt to the need of your customer constantly.

A Quick Note on Handling a Misstep

It happens to the best of brands. To help you recover from this so you can remain a strong brand, consider the following tips:

- If you are in a crisis from a misstep, put out an apology early, repeat it often, and be authentic. Commit to your customers that you will fix the problem.

- Found your brand on ethics. Establish a few principles your brand will operate by so customers can trust your response in a situation will be consistent and fair.
- Build your brand on the obligations of your field, including legal and moral considerations. Adhere to your obligation as a business is your market.
- Uphold a promise. If you say you are going to do or offer something, then you need to do it, even if you realize it is not advantageous to do that.
- Be a part of your community and show your support in return. Give back to those around you.
- Choose your employees wisely so that they accurately represent your brand. Part of emotionally connecting with your brand includes having employees that are human representations of your brand.
- Treat everyone fairly. Keep to the script and treat each customer with a fair approach.
- Stick up for your brand and yourself when you need to. Sometimes a misstep is not your fault. Do not be afraid to defend your position. Other times, you may try to treat a customer fairly, but they will not accept it, taking to public forums to slander your brand. In those situations, it is ok to defend your approach.
- Business is not personal, and neither is a bad review. Not every person will be happy with his or her experience. That is ok, just handle it with fairness and respect.

6

THE SECRET WAY TO MAKE SURE YOUR BRAND IS NEVER SITTING STILL OR FALLING BEHIND

How to Branch Out and Meet New Needs and New Customers

After a while of succeeding with your brand, you are probably starting to get an itch to reach more people. You want to expand what you offer and who you offer it to. As highlighted in the past few chapters, the value of your business relies on the value your customers perceive. It is important to look at the lifetime value and profit potential of your customers and find ways to maximize them. But when you begin to expand, you cannot lose sight of the customers you already have, especially the loyal ones. You need to maintain contact with them while reaching out to a new group of people. The key to attracting these new customers is to offer value to them, as well as keep the value consistent or better for your existing customers. This is the best way to build and keep loyal customers.

An interesting statistic related almost ¾ of a customer's value is increased when you focus on increasing retention by at least 5%. Yet, while 5% seems like a small percentage, you may find yourself wondering how you will obtain that increase. A few of the best ways to do this include offering an informative and valuable newsletter that is free to everyone, by asking the people interacting with your brand for their opinion, investing in strong customer service, and using your online presence for fresh content and promotion.

A newsletter may not sound attractive to your potential and existing customers so it may be relevant to come up with another term for this content. In addition, the content that you offer should be valuable with and without alignment with your brand. This way, it is valuable from the beginning, but can be enhanced with the products or services that you offer. In addition, providing this for free means you can reach a brand group of people, from large businesses to small mom-and-pop shops. A part of this newsletter, or another reach, can ask for people to engage and share with you. It can be in the form of a short survey or even become a part of a focus group. Whatever you decide to do, make it easy and fast to complete. You can also add an incentive for doing it, like access to a special download of more free content or a coupon code for purchase on your site. The information you gather can be related to research of the market you want to target, the experience your customer had while engaging in your brand, or overall satisfaction with their interaction.

The continued focus on customer service must enhance the broader your customer base becomes. When you expand your customers, you also need to expand your customer service team. This is also a good time to look at your processes in place and determine if they are scalable for the increase in customer contact that you can expect. No matter your scripts or policy, you need to make sure each customer is treated respectfully and fairly. If you can ensure that most customers that contact you walk away happy, you can anticipate that they will tell at least three friends about their positive experience, thereby growing your business.

Finally, your online presence needs to be consistent but fresh. The information you provide on your website, for example, should be informative to your current and potential customers. This can include a blog that is a part of your site, or even white papers customers could download if it is relevant to your market. If you are expanding your brand to attract more customers, it could make sense to roll out a new section of your website catered to this new group of people. The added benefit of fresh website content on a regular basis is the increased SEO. On social media, you also need to keep things fresh and promotional. These sites are excellent for sharing links to your website's content, promoting a new campaign or product, or highlighting a customer or employee. This last tip shows a personal side to your brand that customers like to engage with. And as with anything you put online, share it over multiple sites so that most people can interact with your content and share it for you, too.

Customer attraction and retention truly is an art form. It does not need to take a long time to build your base or expand your reach, but it does take time and attention. Do not make the mistake of taking your eye off your current customers as you reach for more. You need to always have one hand on what exists while the other reaches out to invite others in. The tips above are a great way to start this.

Earn and Build Loyalty

Part of this process of continuing your brand's success is

growing your loyal customers. These are the people who will purchase your products at full price, no matter the season or sale, and who go to your brand first when they start considering a purchase. These are also the people that talk about your brand with their friends and family and encourage them to engage with you. Ideally, this group of people should be big enough that they alone can sustain your business. All the other customers are mere "toppings."

The real definition of "customer loyalty" is a measurement of the likelihood or repeat business by a customer. The way of measuring this varies from market to market, but most methods boil down to a basic principle: how many times did one person shop your brand or buy your products since they first engaged with you, or their total lifetime. For example, if a customer has been in your database for four years and has purchased eight times, you can determine if they are more or less loyal than a person who has been in your database for 15 years and purchased 15 times. Regardless of where they fall on your loyalty "line," if a customer is coming back to engage in your brand again, they are a repeat customer, and they are valuable! In fact, repeat customers are the most valuable customers. The purchases may not be the largest, but over time, they may bring revenue to you more than a customer who drops a large amount of cash on a single transaction.

And there is a common thread among all loyal customers in all industries. If they are happy with their experience, they will come back again and spend more money. In addition to the return business, loyal customers bring you additional benefits. One of those benefits is the "free" marketing they do for you. They will share your content online, talk with their friends and family about your brand for you, leave good reviews for you on various sites, and more. Here are a few suggestions on how to reciprocally enhance your loyal customer base. (Reciprocal enhancement means that both you and your customer are benefited by the loyal relationship.)

Suggestion #1: Get to know your people and let them get to know you, too

Think about the time that you met someone, had a nice conversation, and then when you met again in the future, they remembered your name and what you talked about. This is the most powerful method for building customer loyalty. You can mirror this type of personalization with your customers by crafting a personal email or "remembering" their birthday. This illustrates to your customers that you value them and want to know them. With new technology, you can program to send these personalized emails during birthday months or special times of the year, like their anniversary for being a loyal customer!

In addition to getting to know your customers, they want to get to know you, too. Most customers enjoy a personal touch for a brand. Sharing information with your loyal band of customers before anyone else finds out, including the media, is like sharing a secret with your best friends before you tell the rest of the school. Information like a new product launch, a new hire, or even negative information like problems with shipping or delivery is powerful for building strong and loyal customers. You can also put out information to your small group of established, loyal customers to ask for their input before you engage with the rest of your customer base or media. Find ways to talk to your customers to let them know that they are important to you.

Suggestion #2: Develop a loyalty program to reward customers who come back

A lot of brands offer a loyalty rewards card for shopping. The chances are high that if you opened your wallet right now, there would be at least one of those business-card sized punch cards in there somewhere. Starbucks is a great example of a brand that embraced technology and the customer rewards program, offering a way for customers to purchase, earn rewards, and cash in for free products through an app for their mobile device. This app also shares your purchase history and other relevant information with the company, so they always spell your name right (finally!), knows just how you like your drink when your birthday is, and more.

Another option is the branded credit card. You can offer your own private credit program for customers, encouraging them to sign up for your card in exchange for certain benefits like cash back or discounts. This can be a tricky situation, and many customers are wary of committing to a credit situation, but if you are open about the implications and make it worthwhile for your customers, you can get a great commitment from a loyal customer.

Suggestion #3: Make it easy to be a loyal customer

Think of Kindle as a great leader in this, or Amazon, rather. The brand allows you to store your information, like credit card details, so that you can check out with just one click of a button or scan of a fingerprint. Starbucks offers a similar feature through its loyalty app. If the checkout process is lengthy and confusing, especially all the time, you are going to lose customers interest and loyalty. They want to engage with you and move on, so make it easy for them to do that! Another brand to think about is Apple and its iPhone. They make it easy to upgrade your phone because all your information is stored and quickly transferred to your new phone. In addition, the features they adjust on their models are all to make it easier to use their products. For example, the camera can be accessed from the lock screen. The home button can be double tapped for those with smaller hands, and more. Apple does not offer a discount on their products, but because of their transparency regarding the innovation and customer-centric focus they spend time on, they are still able to drive loyalty.

Use automation to yours and your customers benefit as well. There are plenty of methods and technologies you can consider to make the experience easier. Think about a customer who calls your company because something is going wrong. They are not happy. How can you start to make that experience better for them before they even pick up the phone or get on the computer? And once they connect, how can you keep it simple for them? And after the interaction, what is a good follow up strategy? For example, if a customer calls customer service, do they have to navigate an automated and time-wasting system before talking to a person or do you have a system in place that recognizes the phone number and pulls up the account for a person to review when listening to the problem. Is the customer service representative trained on how to handle these types of calls? Do you have a follow-up strategy in place, triggering that representative to give a follow-up call or message to the customer to make sure the problem is solved? If not, it is time to think about it!

. . .

SUGGESTION #4: **Become the expert at what you offer to the market**

Be the best. It is a simple sentence, but a hard action. But if you can become the "go to" expert, customers will be loyal for just that single reason. Think about the brands you like but are just too expensive to shop all the time, and those that are a good price but the quality is lacking. Now think of a brand that is a combination of both. This brand is the "expert" in the market because they figured out how to balance quality with the price for you, their target customer. An example of a brand that is considered the expert in the market is TJ Maxx. They offer affordable, quality merchandise and a consistent brand.

While you are working to become the best, let your customer know it. Show them that you are working to become better and a leader. Take Patagonia, for instance. They have their own competition and are not easily considered the "expert" in outdoor activities, but they show that they are working to be the best through hiring employees that love the outdoors, an innovative business model, and excellent return policies centered on outdoor athletes. Patagonia publicizes that their founder is an outdoor enthusiast, connecting the people personally to the brand. This transparency and clear focus on improving creates a sense of appreciation in your customers.

Suggestion #5: Always look for feedback

If a customer is willing to write a review for you online, they are either really upset about their experience or really happy. If they are happy, there is a great chance they are or will be a loyal customer. And a good review will then serve to drive more potential customers to purchase from you. If you also offer them good service, you will get more reviews, and more customers, and so on. To get the review cycle started, you need to start with great service. This means anyone that interacts with a customer needs to be well trained in how you want them to engage with them. Your technology and processes should be as smooth and easy as possible for your customer. And do not be afraid to ask for feedback. If you resolve a problem with a customer or finish up a sale, ask the customer to give you their opinion of how it went. You can use this information to get better, but also to promote on your online channels, with their permission of course!

You can ask for these reviews in person, online, and through email. It can be an automated message asking for feedback and a review, but if done poorly, it is more of an annoyance than anything else. One way to help balance this is to trigger a series of emails asking for the reviews only after a customer has made a specific number of purchases. This way, you know that they are becoming a more loyal customer. In conjunction with the review, offer a perk, such as a discount or free product.

Advance Your Successful Brand through Social Media

You can advance your brand with these customer-focused strategies, but there are more general advancement strategies to consider, such as working with marketing tools. One of the most powerful tools today is social media. And the added perk of this is it is either free or low cost when compared with more traditional outlets. In this current climate, the identity of a brand is tied to its social media presence. This is because it engages your customers and audience in a personal way, but also raises awareness. If used well, it can also establish trust and loyalty. The engagement on your social accounts is what is used to determine your success with the outlet. The more you get people to engage on your pages, the better you are doing. This means that you should not be looking at the number of people that, "like" or "follow" your page, but how often those that engage with your page interact with it. In fact, the more people that follow your accounts but do not engage, the worse you are doing.

Clicks on your URLs, re-tweets, shares, comments, and likes are just a few examples of customer engagement. This is vital to the success of your account, but it is not always easy. Part of the problem is that these sites are designed for personal use, not commercial, so all the algorithms support the personal user experience, not the business side (A great example of a brand keeping their focus on their customer rather than the business). Also, the general landscape of social space is challenging for a business to navigate successfully. You need to be on top of the changes and techniques for saturating and reaching your customer.

There are some tried-and-true methods for effectively engaging on social media. Of course, not all are relevant to your business and cannot just be blindly applied to each approach, but they are a great place to start. First and foremost, you need to be relevant. More and more users are adopting social media as part of their daily lives. And when on there, an incredible amount of messaging is finding its way in front of them. Most of the messages are ignored, not because they cannot solve the customer's problem or the brand is not good, but because it is not engaging or relevant to them. It simply does not stand out. The best way to stand out is to be interesting. Keep your content consistent with your brand, but relevant to your customer. Fans of your business can be segmented and targeted through Facebook, for example. This means you can watch the analytics of your page and understand your social audience. From there, you can create content that speaks to them directly. You can even use geo-targeting or language to gate the post for even more concentration.

And while you are developing the content to this targeted group, make sure the content you are putting out and responding to have an authentic voice. You are a person after all! Reply like one. Social media is about that, being social. When your customers see that you are more than just a brand, they are more likely to feel connected to you, and therefore, more loyal. But the length of time between a comment and a response is critical. Try to reply quickly to an engagement from a customer. And highlight information shared by your users. You can even reward the user for posting content on your page.

When the opportunity presents itself, use your social platforms to delight your customers or give them a good surprise. Offering something unexpected to your audience fosters an emotional response with your customers that you may not get through other channels. For example, if you see that one of your customers is struggling with an illness, you can surprise them with a get-well-soon gift or card delivered to the hospital they are at. Or if you notice someone is celebrating an anniversary, you can coordinate a special treat for them with the hotel. This kind of action shows the customer and others that see this, that you care about them and are paying attention to their lives. In addition, it creates the impression that you go above in beyond when it does not directly impact your bottom line, and customers are more likely to become loyal in this situation.

Become a part of the conversations on social media. One way you can do this is by using hashtags. This is a great way to see what is going on in the market. Be careful here, though. You do not want to overuse hashtags! Consider developing a tag specifically for your own brand, and use it with more generic ones. This helps increase brand awareness and exposure. The only exception is that on Instagram, you do want to go hashtag-crazy to help improve your visibility. Another way to become a part of the conversation is by partnering with influencers. These people or other brands can help you gain visibility and credibility through a third-party. Most of the time, you have to pay well to get a spotlight on their accounts, but it can be money well spent if you get the right collaboration. It is important that the message being shared on their account is consistent with your brand as well as relevant to their audience and yours. This takes some time to master.

And after you put anything up on social, you need to conduct a post-mortem. Analyze how it did, measure its success, and learn what to do and not to do next time. You need to know the result of your efforts so you can decide what is worth it and what is not. There are a lot of opportunities to make mistakes on social media because of how it is designed. This means that one of the best approaches to learning social media is simply to put things out there and see what happens. But never forget to dissect the results to learn how to approach your next move. And, make sure that whatever you decide, that you do not make it a blind-copy approach. The landscape constantly changes and so must your approach. You need to evolve with the changes so you can accurately advance your brand.

Advance Your Successful Brand through Traditional Media

While social media has gained notoriety and importance in brand strategy, there is still a place for the more traditional mediums as well. Television, specifically, is still at the center of a consumer's world. Yes, online television and on-demand services are a competition to traditional cable or network TV, but this "linear" television still wins out the majority when compared to digital sources. "Linear" TV is real-time, historically broadcast content. It is still an important source of entertainment across the world. A recent estimate shows that linear is over 2 ½ times viewed more per day than digital. Digital includes on-demand and streamed content.

This can explain why linear television advertising still sees returns and is still effective at reaching an audience. Using traditional media still holds a strong presence in brand awareness and image. And with the advancement of technology for advertising on linear television, you can now address a specific audience typically watching a specific channel or show. What was impossible before is now vital to your success with traditional media. For example, many homes are digital or smart homes. They share information openly about the household family dynamics, ethnicity, and income that can all be used for targeted marketing strategies through traditional sources. Now you do not have to waste time and resources on an audience that does not have an interest in your brand. "Addressable" TV marketing is rising and estimated to continue to do so as more and more companies and brands are embracing the new opportunity in "old" media.

Expanding Your Already-Successful Brand

Below is a quick list of things you should do to keep your brand growing and expanding, even after you have found your success.

1. Always look at the heart of your brand. Evaluation is always an ongoing process.
2. Keep your current audience by staying on communication with them, even when you start bringing in new customers.
3. Understand your costs and where you need to spend more or less for your business to grow. You do not want to waste money on something that does not benefit your business, but on the other hand, you need to be willing to re-invest in the growth.
4. Consider launching your new ideas or products softly, so it does not make a big noise, especially if it falls. Doing this means less embarrassment if something is not quite right yet.
5. Do not forget your past; learn from it. As you prepare to continue to expand, look back at what was a success and what failed for you and determine how you will use this information to grow.

CONCLUSION

Thank you for reading through to the end of *Brand Identity: Building Your Breakthrough Business with Branding Pays.* I hope it was informative and offered a variety of applicable tools that you can apply to your business today. Hopefully, the techniques are valuable to your advancement towards your goals, whatever they may be.

The next step you need to take is to take an honest and deep look into your brand as it stands today. Maybe you are just developing it, and it is nothing more than a vision in your mind. Or maybe you have a brand that has been around for a century with a loyal band of customers. No matter where you fall in this spectrum, take the time to dig into the identity of your brand. Look internally to your employees for information, and externally to the marketplace. Do focus groups, surveys, polls, meetings, or anything else you think is necessary to figure out what you are putting out there and decide if it really aligns with what you want it to do.

What you want your brand to accomplish is a very important

question to answer. It is at the core of developing your identity, but you must also explore how you want your customer to perceive your brand. Put words around the impression you want your customers to get any time they engage in your brand. From this starting point, you can begin to identify the opportunities in your existing brand. Look for areas that are not jiving with what you want to do and what you want people to experience. Sometimes, this means adjusting your outward strategy, and other times, it means adjusting your internal culture. And for some, maybe it is adjusting both! And of course, what works today, may not work tomorrow. This means this process is ongoing, no matter the size or age of your brand.

Your vision for your brand may not be to make it globally recognized, but you do still want people to know who you are and set yourself apart from the competition. You also want to make sure customers sense that you are a reliable and experienced brand that can fulfill their needs. If you have a large brand or goals or something more niche and boutique, you can benefit from a strong brand identity. It can help you set premium prices, establish the perception of quality, and build loyalty. And so much more! If you are struggling in developing your identity, go back to chapter one to review the steps and suggestions on how to find your true identity and come up with something meaningful to your target market.

If you have a good start to your identity or have something established but want to build upon it, do not forget the importance of your customers. Are your messages, policies, and culture business-centered or customer-centric? If you notice that something is in place that is for the benefit of the brand and not the customer, think now about ways to change that. You want to get people to look at you and want to engage. A lot of this has to do with good marketing strategies, but it all boils down to understanding and mindfully communicating with your customers. Read over chapter two again if you want a refresher on how you can emulate some of the more successful marketing strategies and avoid some of the "bad" ones.

Your customers are the reason you have a brand in the first place. Without them, you are just a fancy business card and unused website. To show them how much you value them, first you need to figure out who they are and how you can solve their problems; not all their problems, but a problem that you can offer a solution to. This is critical to a successful brand strategy. Check out chapter three again for more ideas on how to do this, if you find that it is the area you need to pay attention to now. Keeping your focus on the customer and getting to know them help raise your awareness with them and move your brand into a more mature stage.

The lifecycle of your customers is part of this understanding. All customers go through a cycle of behavior, but where they are at when they engage in your brand or what makes them decide to purchase from you and not your competition is a fine art and balance. Part of the beauty of technology is that now customers have access to all their options. They can quickly research who offers what they need and at what price. If you do not stand out to them during this process, you may never convert them from a browser to a buyer. But on the other hand, if you can offer them something unexpected, such as a solution that goes beyond the customer's expectation, you can hook them. Of course, there are a variety of strategies to engage a customer while browsing, which you can review in chapter four, as well as strategies to get them to commit to a sale, which you can review in chapter five.

As you work and tweak and review and tweak some more, you will be making informed decisions to advance your brand. You do not want to put time and effort into setting up a great brand identity to let it become stagnant or fall behind the competition. You do not need to increase your business if you want to stay a boutique brand, but you do need to advance your brand. This may mean building your loyal customer base. Or maybe you do want to expand to a new target market with new products. This may mean making small changes to your brand that reflects the new approach while still keeping the identity consistent. Ideas shared in the final chapter are designed to help you navigate these waters to continue to grow, even after you have experienced success.

Now that you have a great place to start, a good understanding of who you are, what you want, and what areas of your brand you are going to focus on to advance forward, start pulling in key stakeholders to find out how you are going to pull it all together. If you have not brought in marketing, customer service, etc., now is the time to do it. Tell them what you want to do for your brand and how you see it taking your business into the future. Secure their buy-in and get them to help trickle it down through their departments. After all, the best place to create meaningful change is from within, and this is the time and place to start. You can develop a brand that turns heads and boost the bottom line! Come back to this guide any time you need a reminder that you can do it.

Finally, if you found this book useful in any way, a review on Amazon is always appreciated!

www.ingramcontent.com/pod-product-compliance
Lightning Source LLC
Chambersburg PA
CBHW021832170526
45157CB00007B/2781